ORLANDO

A Journey in Pictures through Central Florida

Photography by
David Cotton

Design by
Cindy Burkett

A publication of The Orlando Sentinel
Sentinel Communications Company
Orlando/1989

Copyright © 1989
Sentinel Communications Company
633 North Orange Avenue
Orlando, Florida 32801
All rights reserved

Photography by David Cotton
Design by Cindy Burkett
(Burkett Advertising Associates)
Text by Joan McCain

Special Thanks To
The Orlando Sentinel
Camera Department

Photo Contributors:
Cypress Gardens
Disney-MGM Studios
Patti Bose
Sea World
Southern Ballet Theatre
Universal Studios Florida
Walt Disney World

Printed in the United States by R.R. Donnelley
First edition 1989
Revised second edition, 1991
ISBN 0-941263-22-3

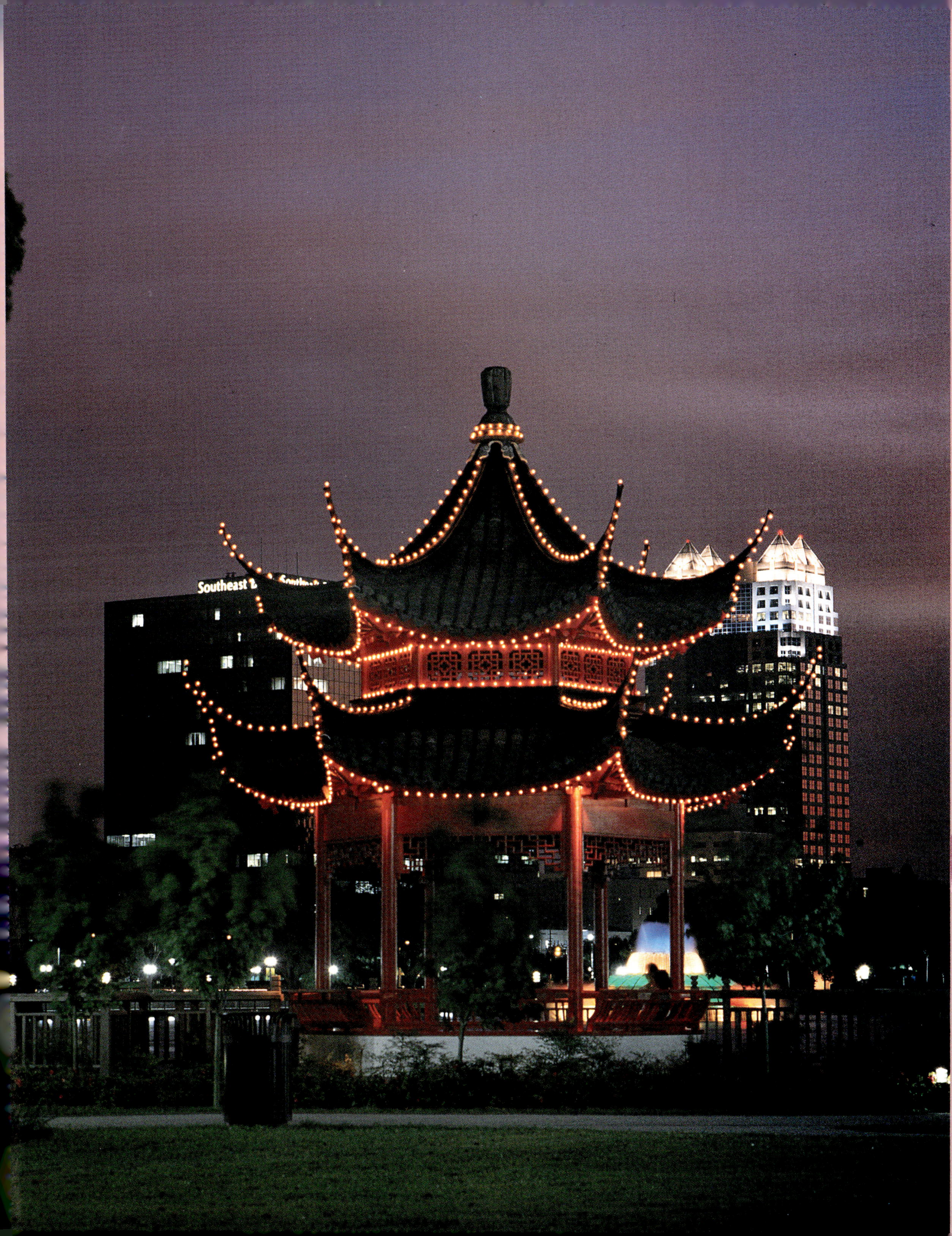
Southeast

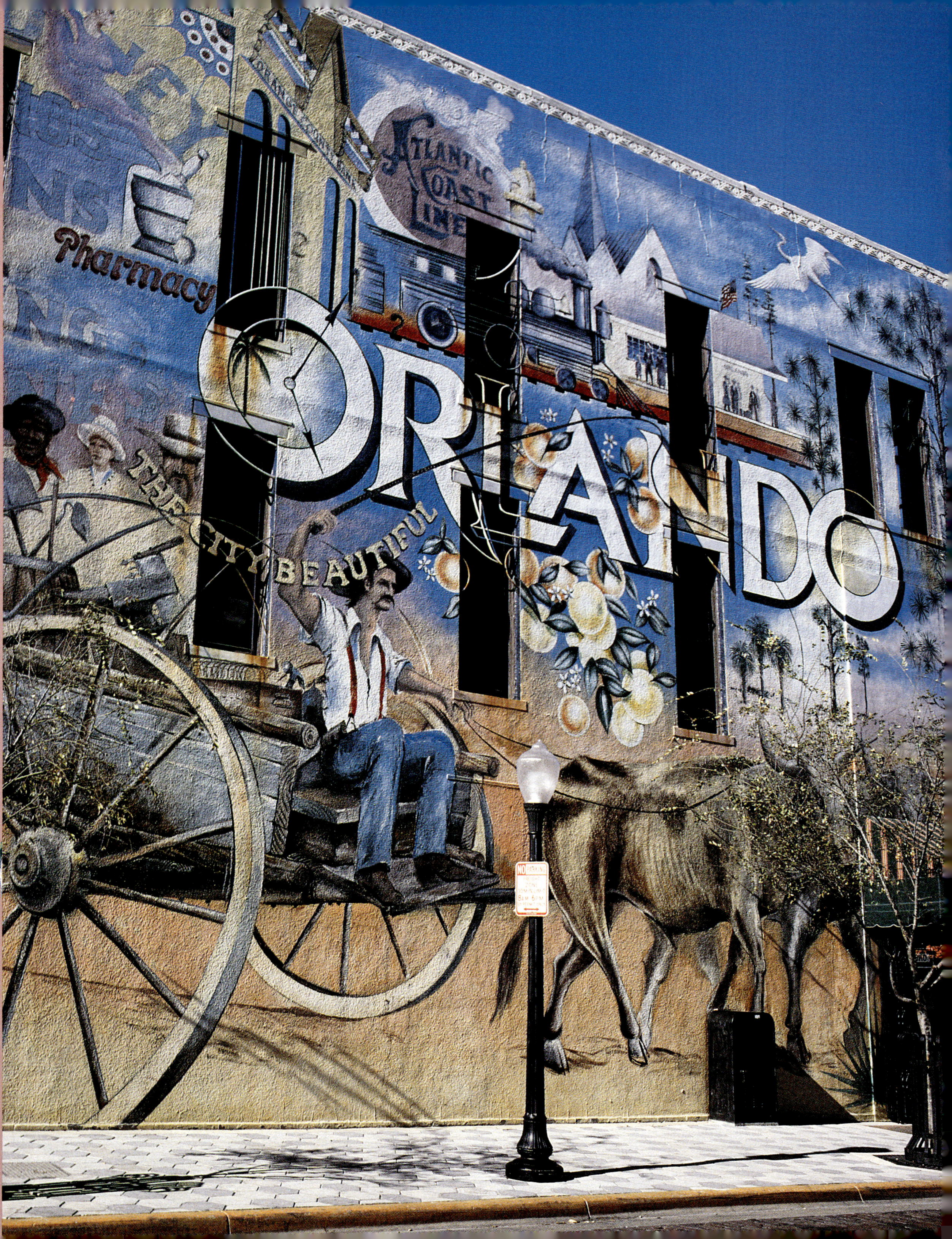
Pharmacy
ATLANTIC COAST LINE
ORLANDO
THE CITY BEAUTIFUL

From the Mayor...

"Exciting" is the word I would use to describe how it feels to be in Orlando today. Orlando is a dynamic, vibrant city that is changing before our eyes.

Our downtown is undergoing a renaissance. We're adding new shops and restaurants. And new office buildings are giving the city a distinctive skyline all its own.

Orlando is a wonderful place to live and work but a terrific city for fun after hours. What other community witnesses the birth of a killer whale one day and plays host to the opening of a world-class movie studio the next? Only Orlando!

We are a city on the move — absolutely. But a community that values its great natural beauty and its tranquil moments away from the bustle of business and commerce. We are parks and arts and quiet neighborhoods.

The following pages capture it all: our excitement, our lifestyle, our attractions and our beauty. All of the elements that have given Orlando the title "The City Beautiful" are here. If a picture is worth a thousand words, this book speaks volumes about our community.

Enjoy!

Best wishes,

Bill Frederick

Bill Frederick

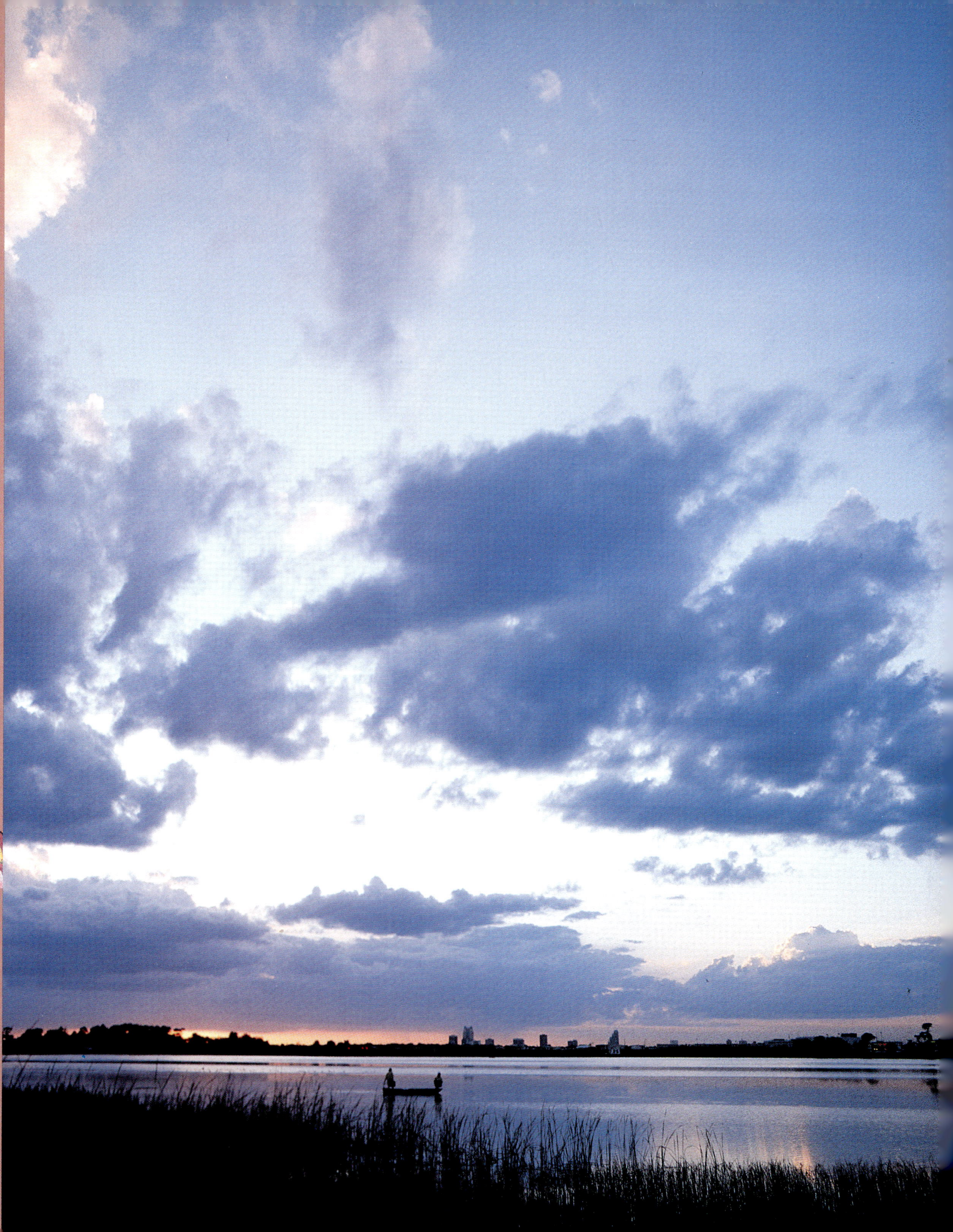

Contents

A Skyline On The Move
Highrises □ Streetscapes

A Day In The Life
Neighborhoods □ Daily routines □ Local traditions

Out On The Town
Festivals □ Attractions □ Parks □ Noteworthy spots

All Things Bright And Beautiful
Wildlife □ Parks □ Waterways

Nowhere To Go But Up
High technology □ Manufacturing □ Workplaces

Gliding into morning at Lake Eola.

Looking for the morning sun at Lake Eola.

Olympia Place from Lake Adair in College Park.

Three swans near the fountain at Lake Eola.

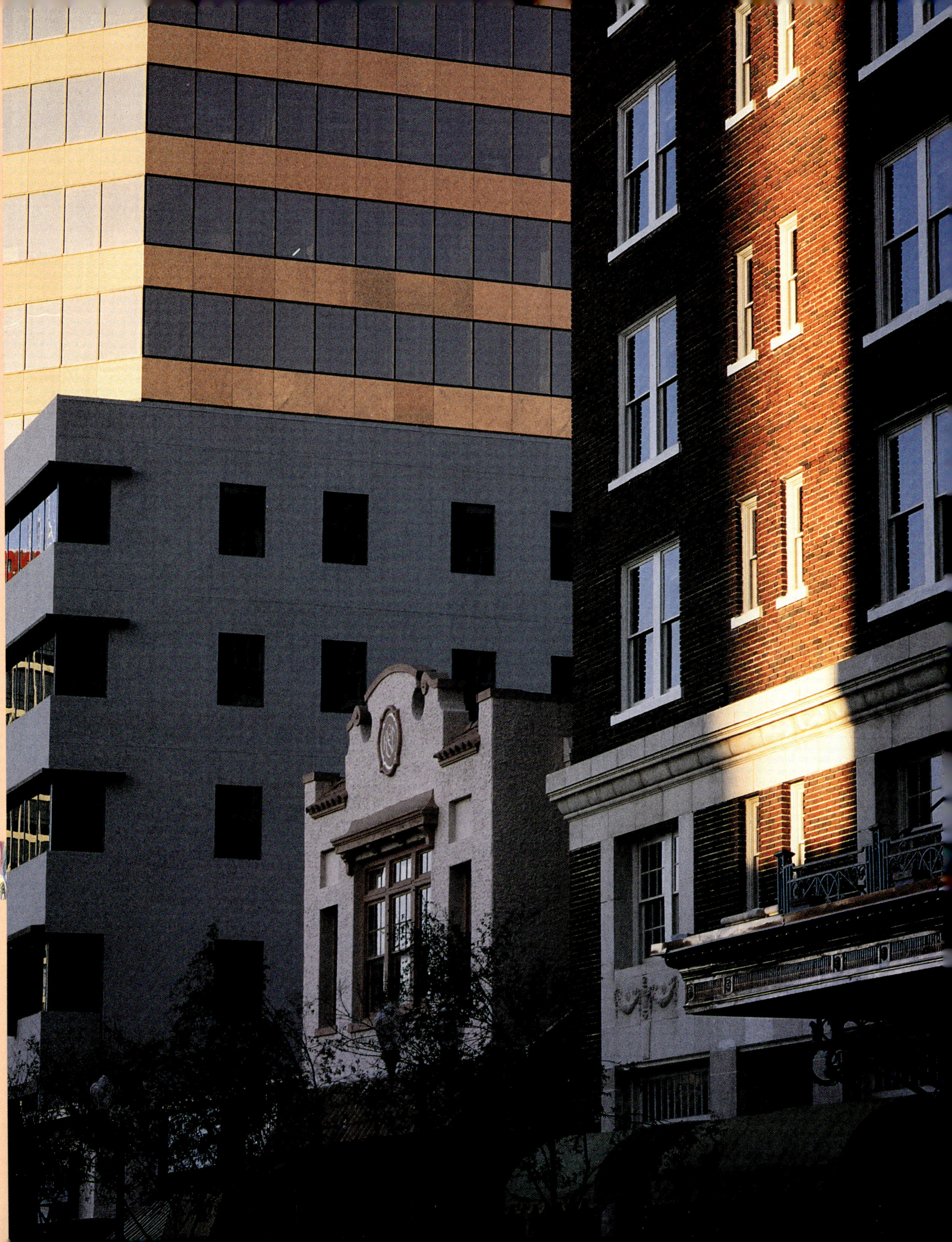

A Skyline On The Move

Explore downtown Orlando and take in the sights. Compare the historic, preserved architecture with the sleek, modern office buildings glistening in the Central Florida sun.

The restaurants, shops and offices — both old and new — are surrounded by lakes, trees and year-round blooms of color. All are enjoyed by residents and visitors who come to the city's core for working, playing, shopping and relaxing.

Given Orlando's ever-changing skyline, change is the only constant downtown.

The look of downtown architecture is as varied as the windows themselves.

Lake Ivanhoe's view
of the downtown skyline.

**Olympia Place
has sky-level seating.**

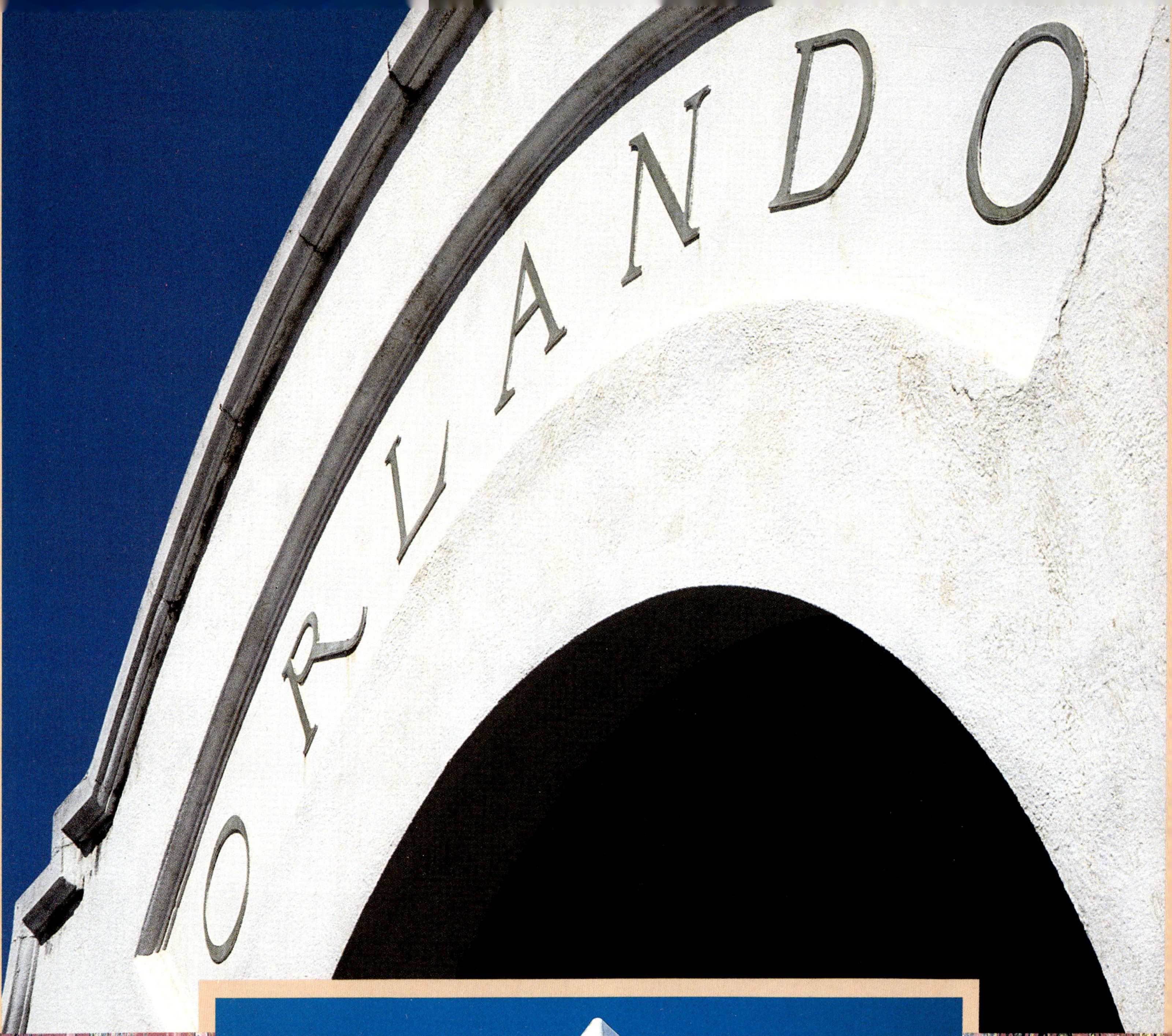
ORLANDO
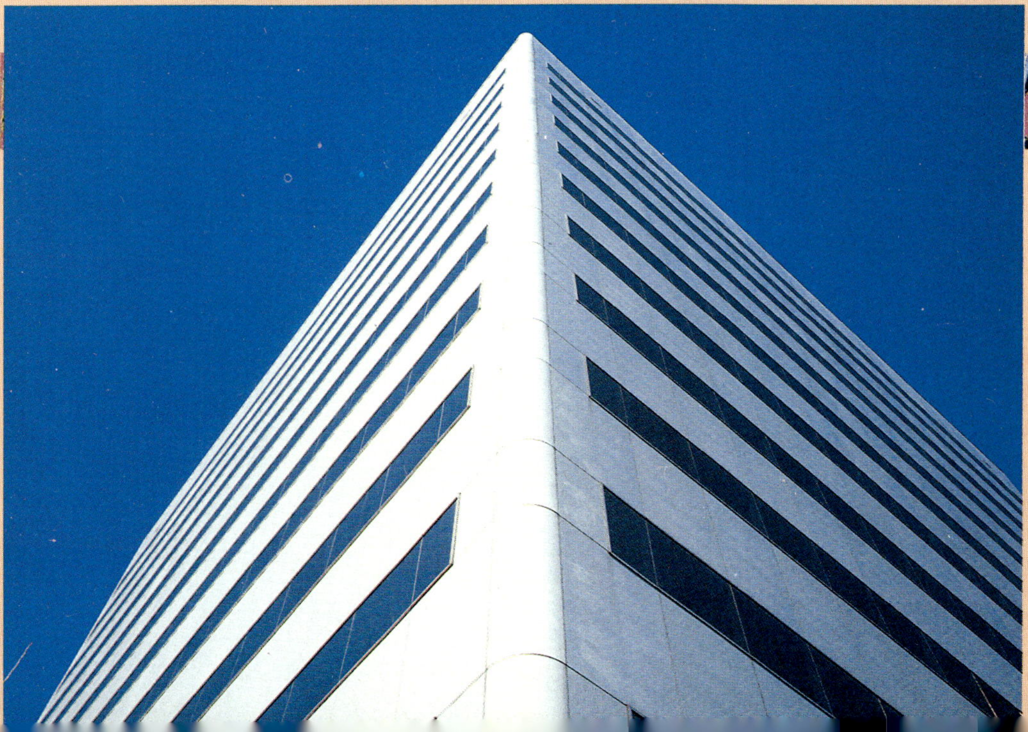

Orlando gateway at downtown's Amtrak station. □ Steel and glass reach for the sky.

SunBank Center is Orlando's tallest building, rising 35 stories. □ The downtown Amtrak station with its revitalized look.

ORLANDO UTILITIES
FIRSTATE
First Union
Barnett Bank
FEDERAL

The East-West Expressway crosses Lake Lucerne at south Orange Avenue. Nearby, a turret at Church Street Station.

A juxtaposition of architectural detail on Orange Avenue. □ Sunset dances on a Centroplex fountain and duPont Centre.

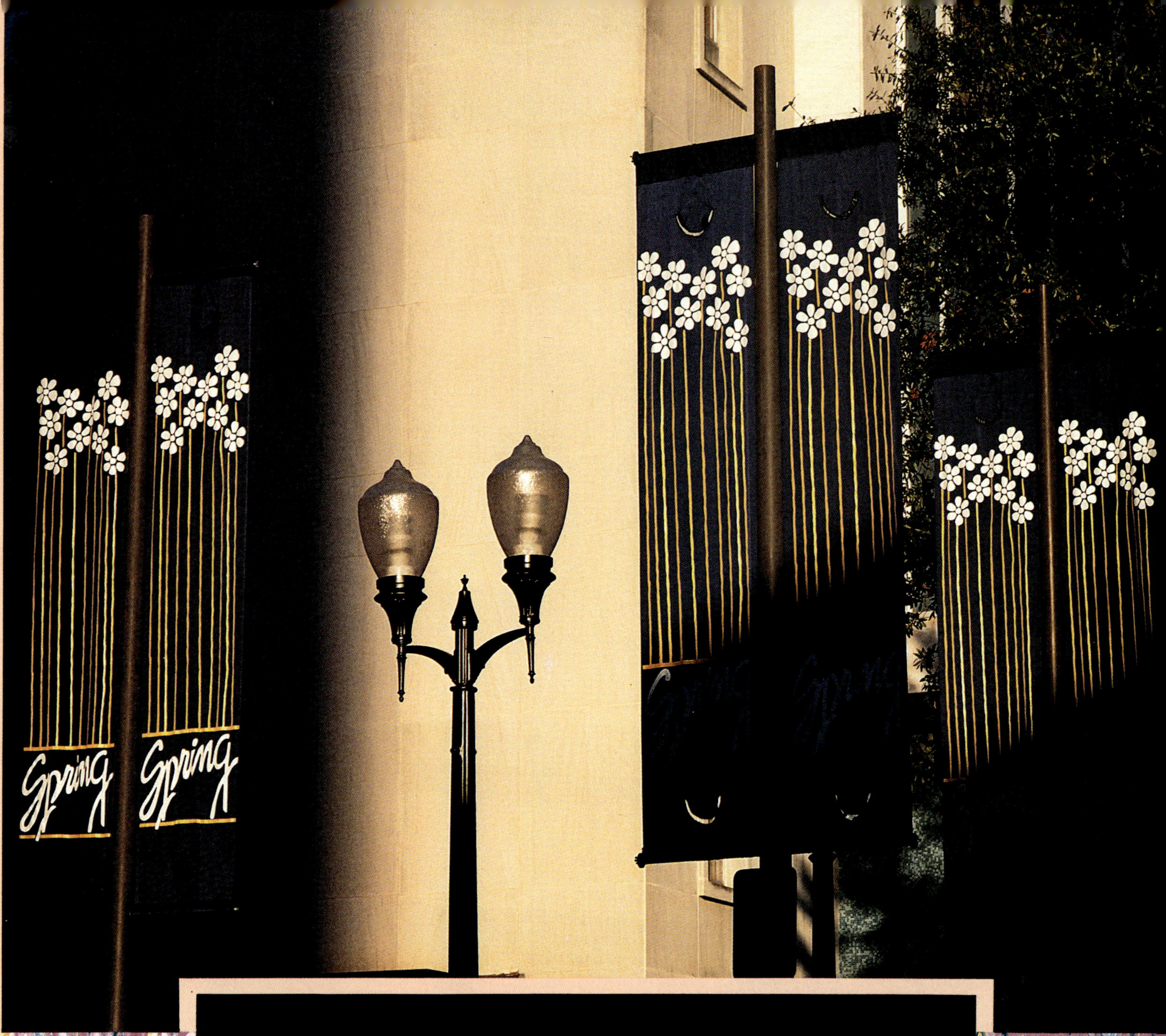
Spring
Spring

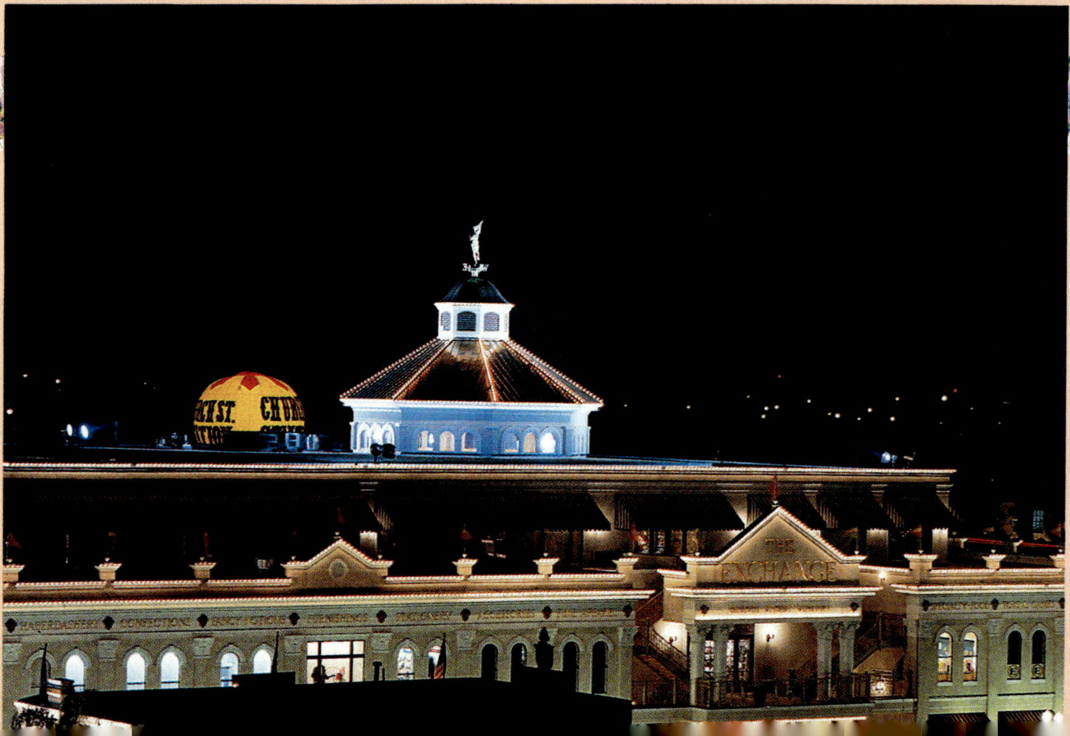
THE
EXCHANGE

A sign of the seasons changing on the streets of downtown Orlando. □ Signs of nightlife at Church Street Station downtown.

Eclectic architecture gives downtown a look all its own. Brick streets, renovation of historic areas, and new developments add to its character.

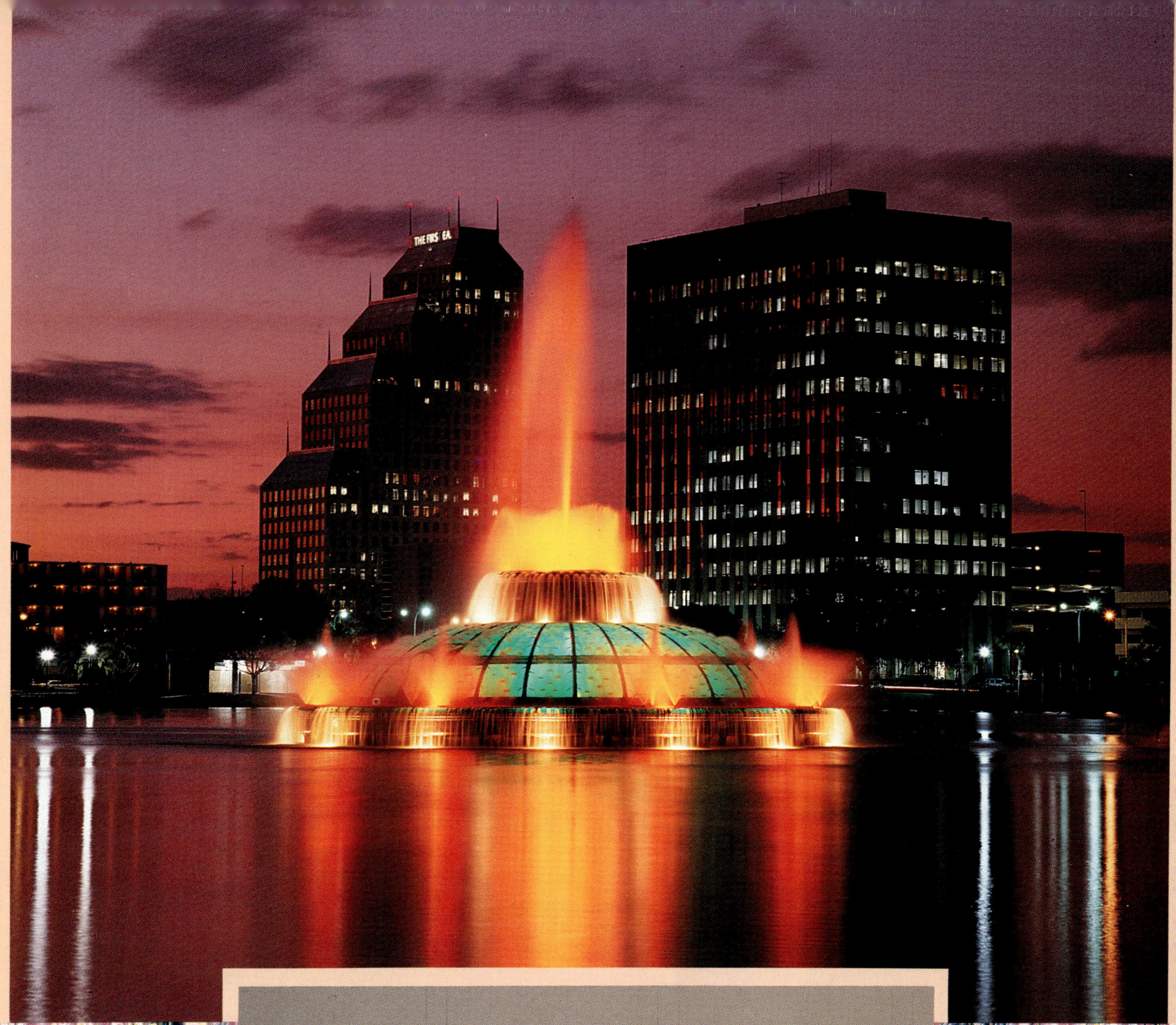

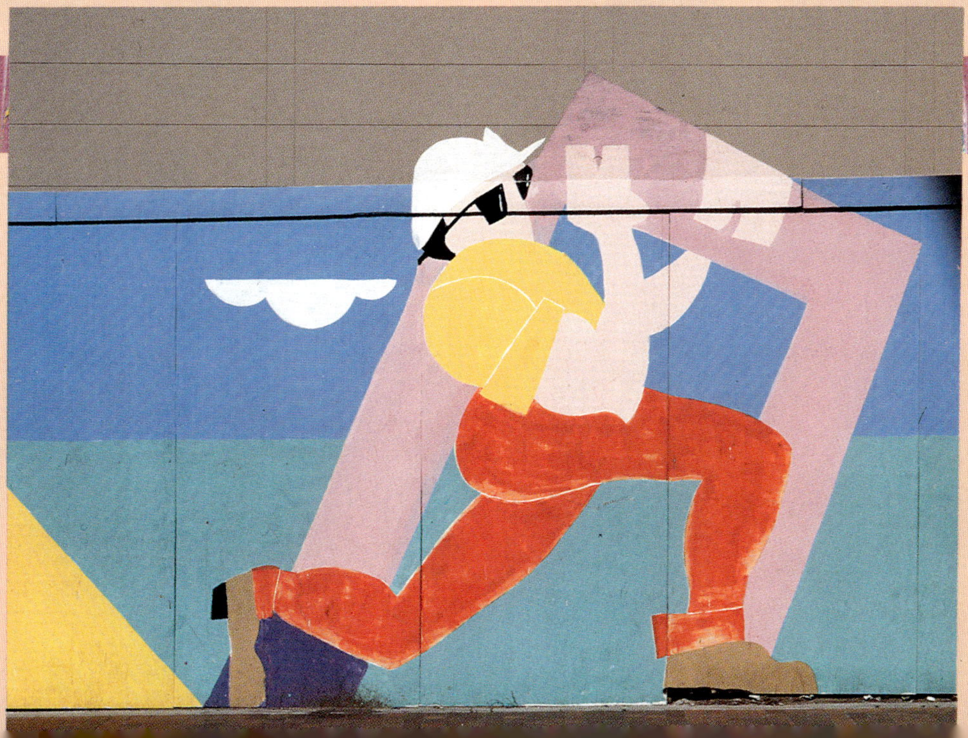

The Eola Fountain is Orlando's trademark and casts even more dancing lights against the downtown skyline. □ Art meets function with the fence around SunBank Center's construction site.

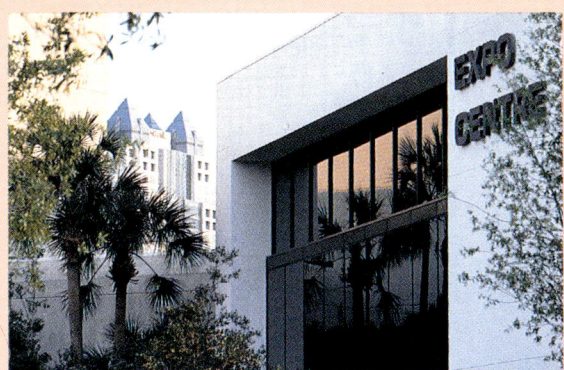

Bob Carr Performing Arts Centre on Livingston Street. Orlando Public Library on Central Boulevard. □ Window washing downtown. Expo Centre at Centroplex. Downtown's First United Methodist Church. □ Southeast Bank Building on Pine Street.

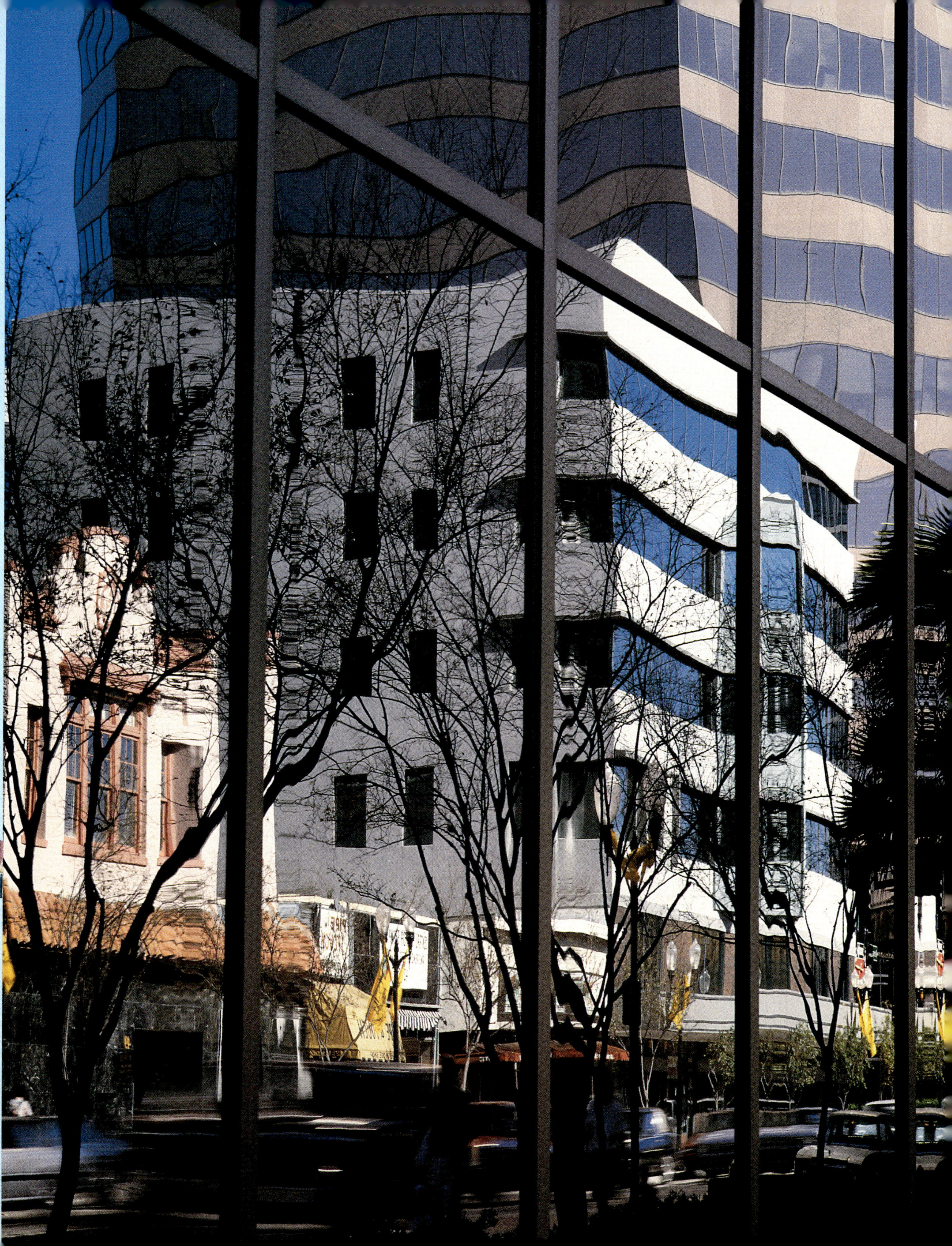

A Day In The Life

Morning finds Orlando already on the move, getting ready for school or on the way to work. Lunch is under the trees or disguised as a street party. Midday breezes mean family play-time fun. Afternoons are made for strolls in botanical parks. Striking evening sunsets happen so frequently they could almost be taken for granted.

Evening choices fit any mood — from first-class entertainment to star gazing from a front porch swing.

There's a day full of choices and enjoyment every hour on the hour.

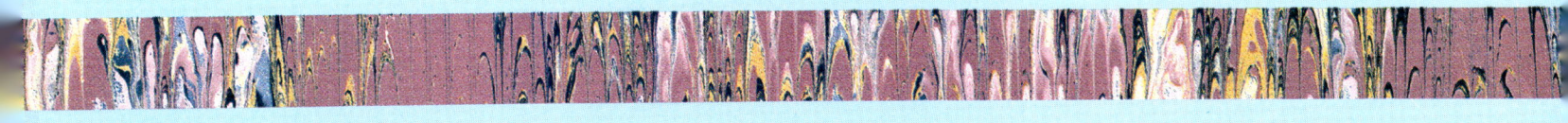

Sunny skies, tree-lined streets and a city on the move reflect Orlando's daily routine.

A historic facade at the Callahan Neighborhood Center.

Lunch time at Eola Park.

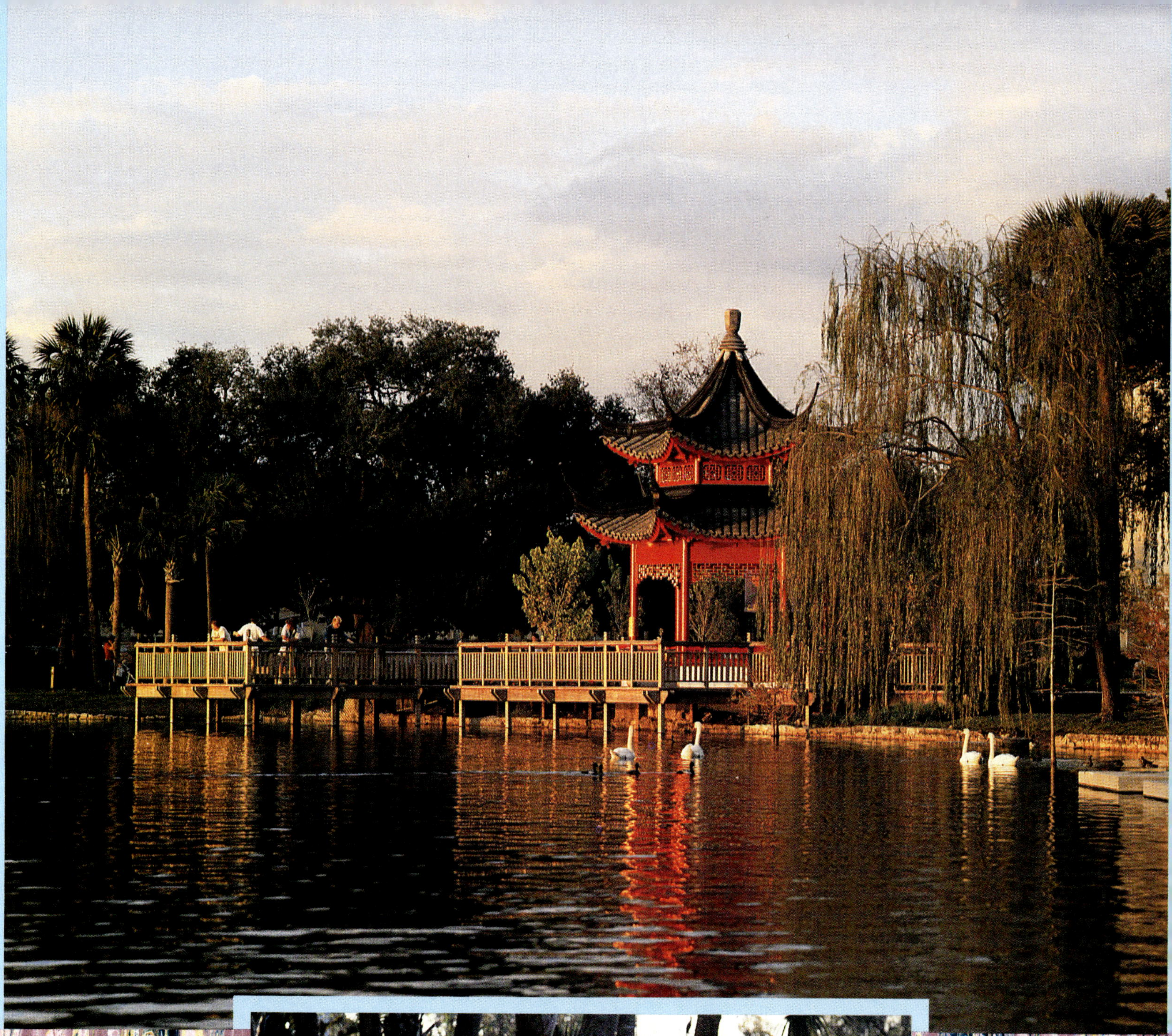

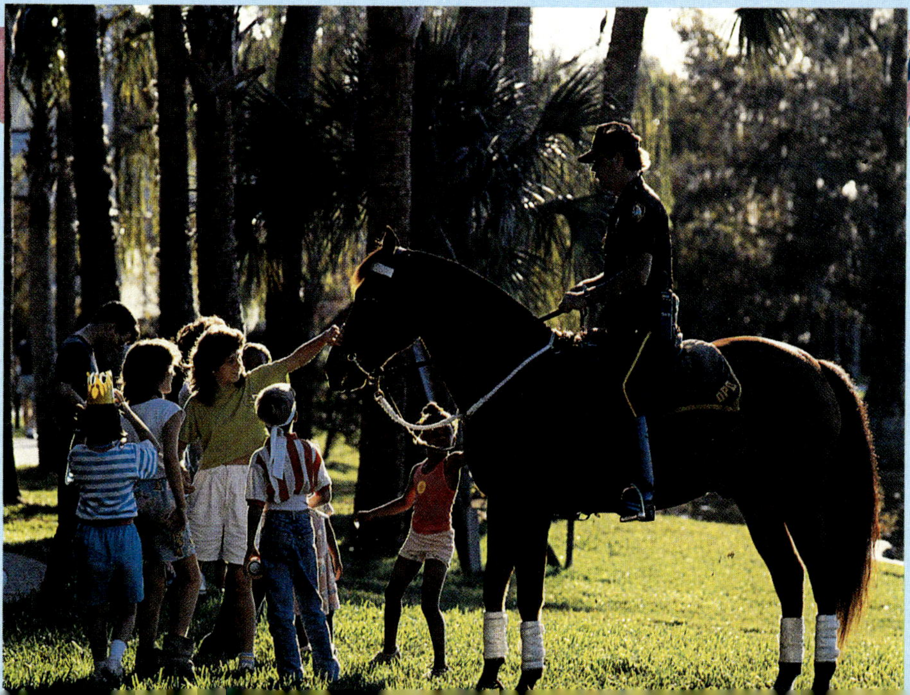

The Chinese ting at Eola Park is one of several scenic points around the manicured lakeshore. □ Orlando Police Department's latest patrol car makes some new friends.

Church Street Station is at the center of downtown nightlife. □ Businesspeople lunch under the trees at SunBank Plaza. Festival Fridays, held at noon in the courtyard of Barnett Plaza, feature music, entertainment and plenty to hold everyone's attention.

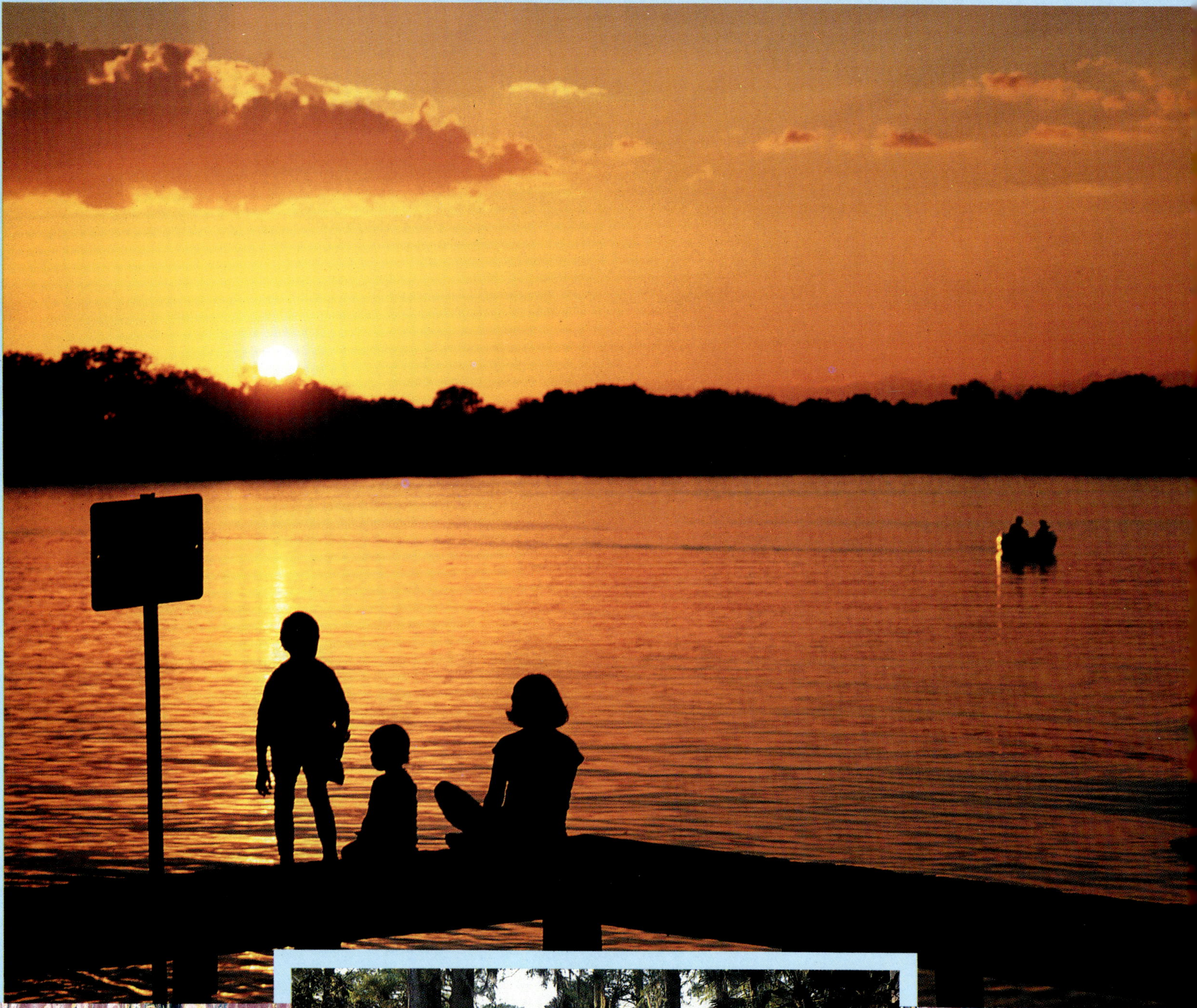

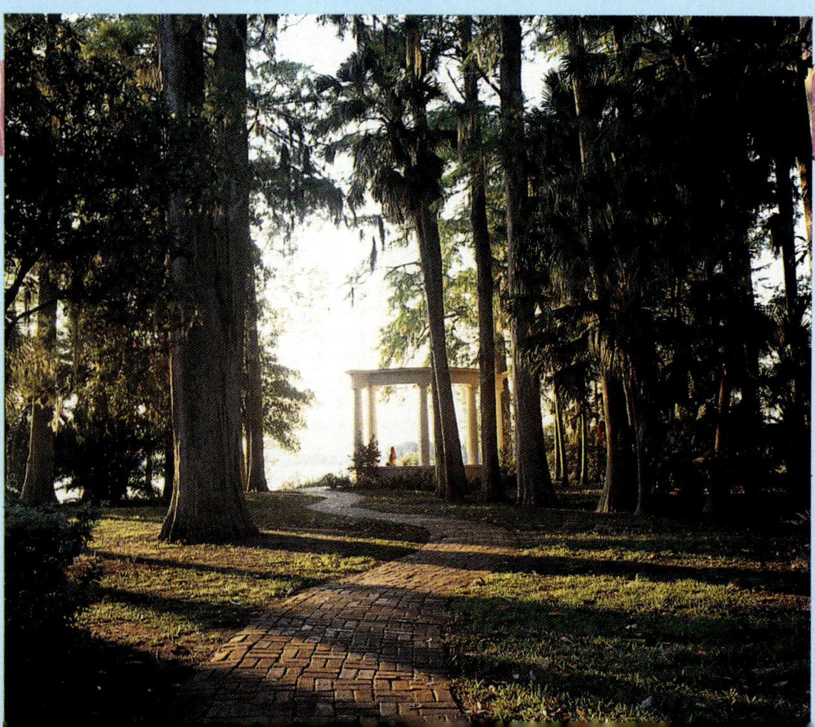

Sunset watching could easily become a favorite pastime in Central Florida — as it is for these children on Lake Underhill. □ Kraft Azalea Gardens on Lake Maitland in Winter Park has many scenic spots for strolling or contemplating.

Leu House Museum at Leu Gardens preserves the furnishings and appointments of a well-to-do 1900s Florida family. □ Downtown's Lake Cherokee historic district. Play time at Eola Park. Saturday morning volleyball at Gaston Edwards Park on Lake Ivanhoe. □ Dickson Azalea Park near downtown.

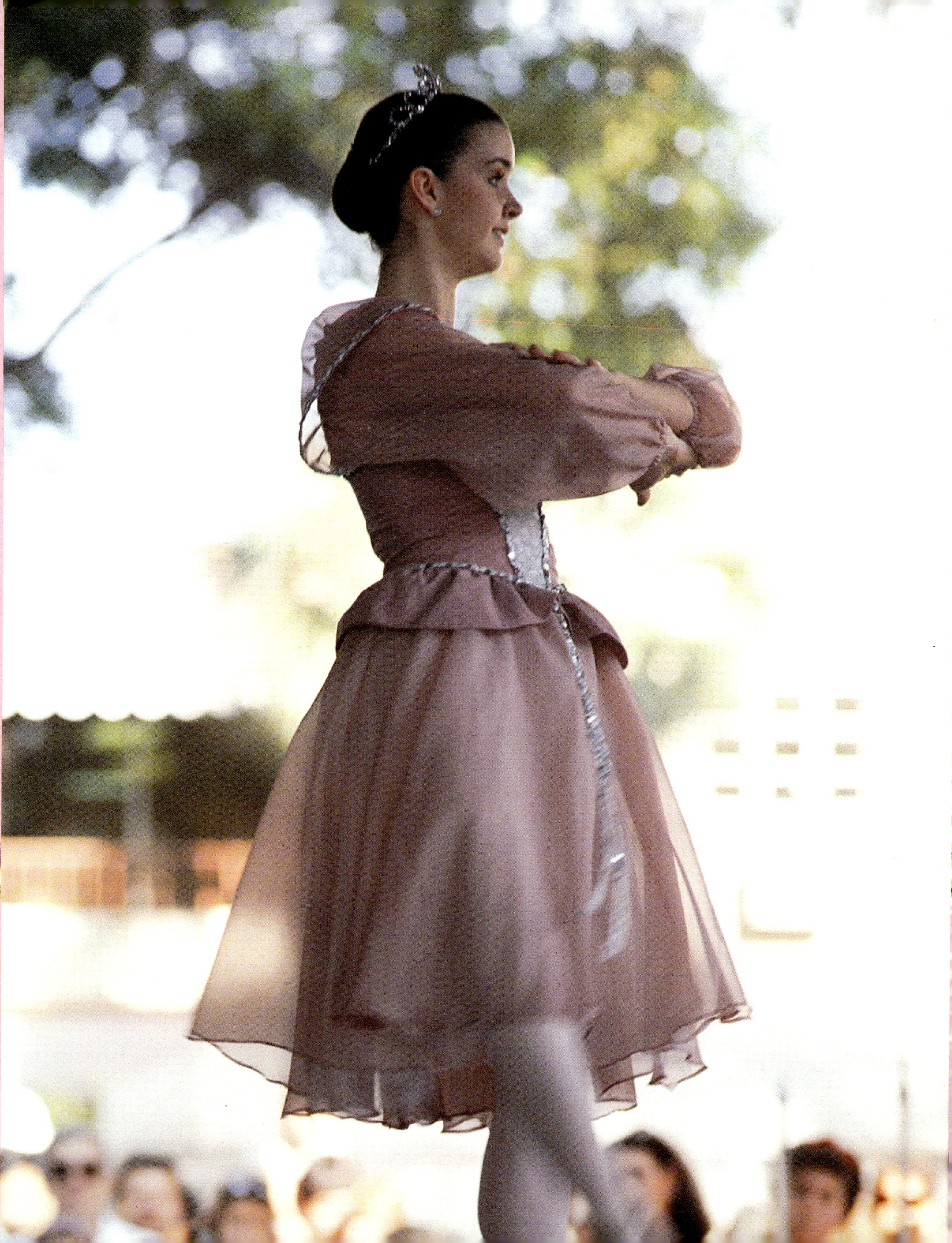

Out On The Town

There is always something to do in Orlando. Without a glance at a social calendar, there are plenty of beaches to enjoy and all kinds of water sports. Annual festivals are traditional celebrations. Professional sports bring big league action home. The ballet, opera, fine art museums, theater and a symphony orchestra round out Orlando's cultural palette.

And of course, Central Florida hosts millions of tourists each year who come for warmth, southern hospitality and world-class tourist attractions.

Southern Ballet Theatre dancer performs at Winter Park Sidewalk Art Festival.

Clemson Tigers celebrate a touchdown at the Florida Citrus Bowl.

A new perspective on the entertainment at Strawberry Spring Festival.

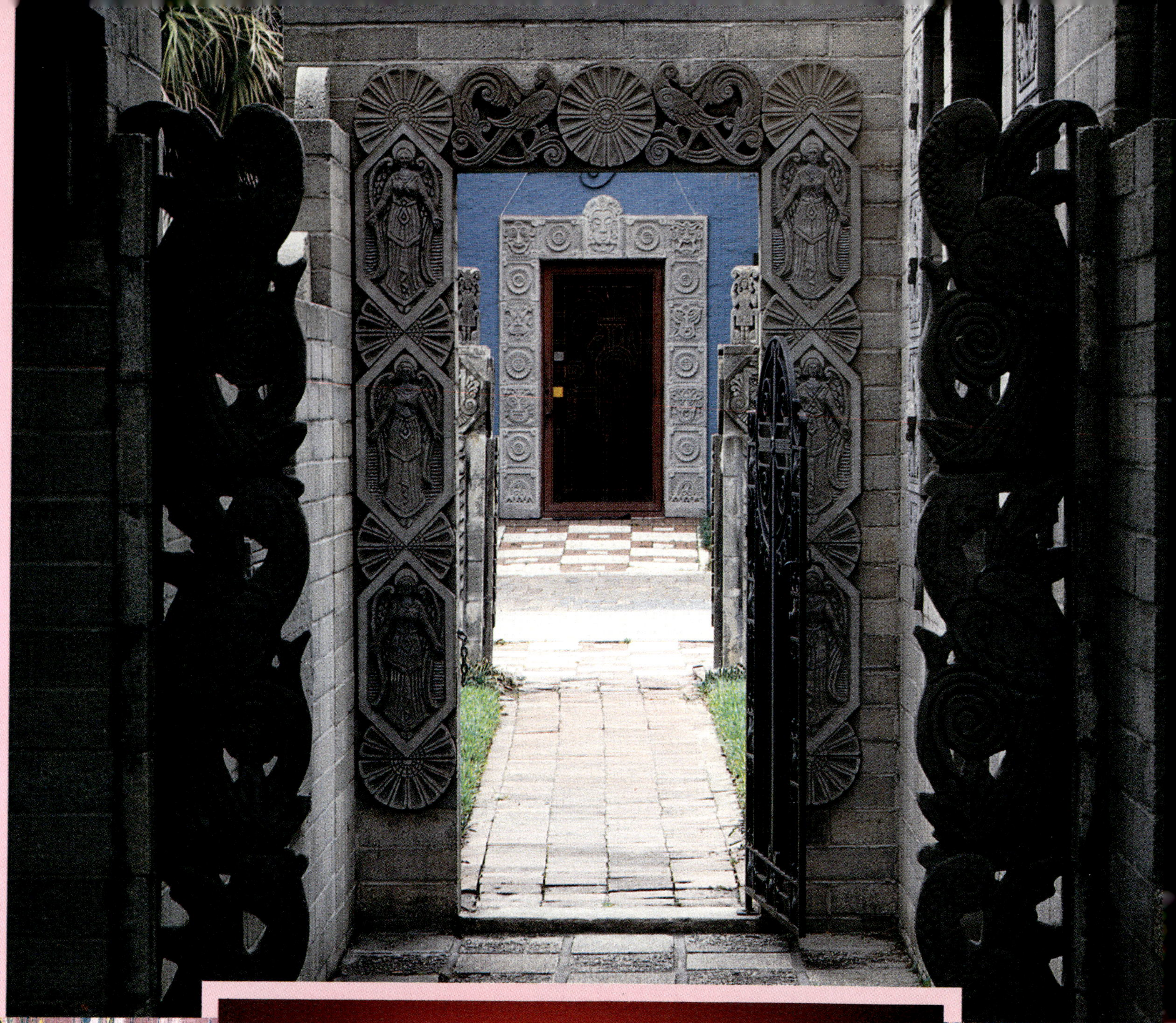

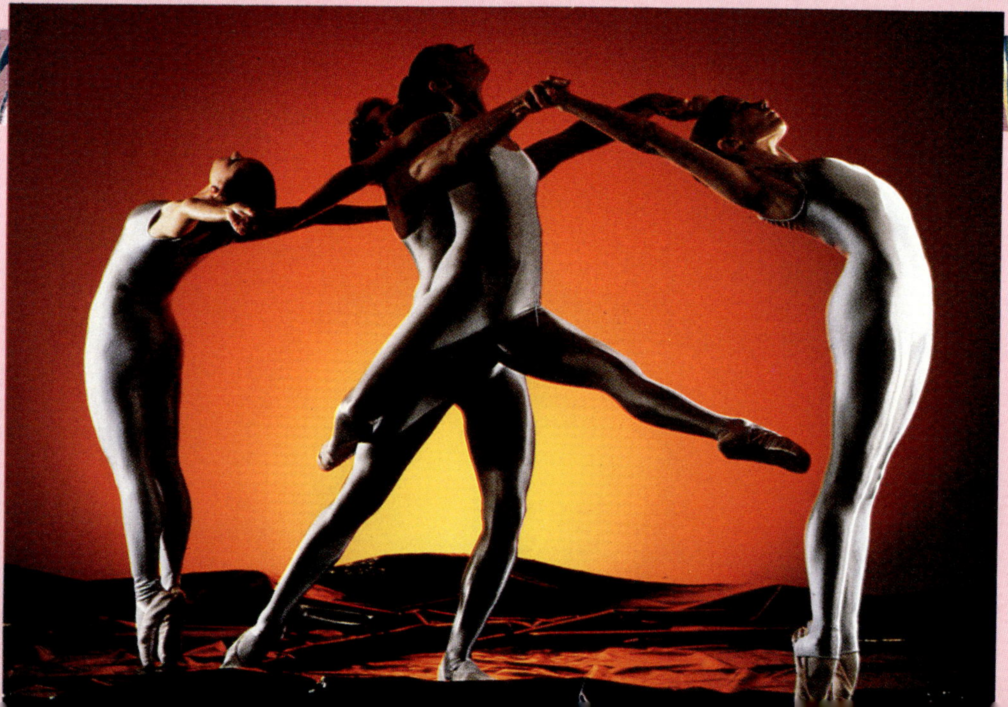

The Maitland Art Center is a state historic site, due to artist Andre Smith's architectural designs from 1938. □ Southern Ballet Theatre brings traditional and contemporary dance to Central Florida. □ The Florida Symphony Orchestra plays at Loch Haven Park. Throughout its nine-month season, the Symphony, under musical director Kenneth Jean, also plays at Bob Carr Performing Arts Centre downtown.

Southern Ballet Theatre Photo
By Patti Bose, © Patti Bose

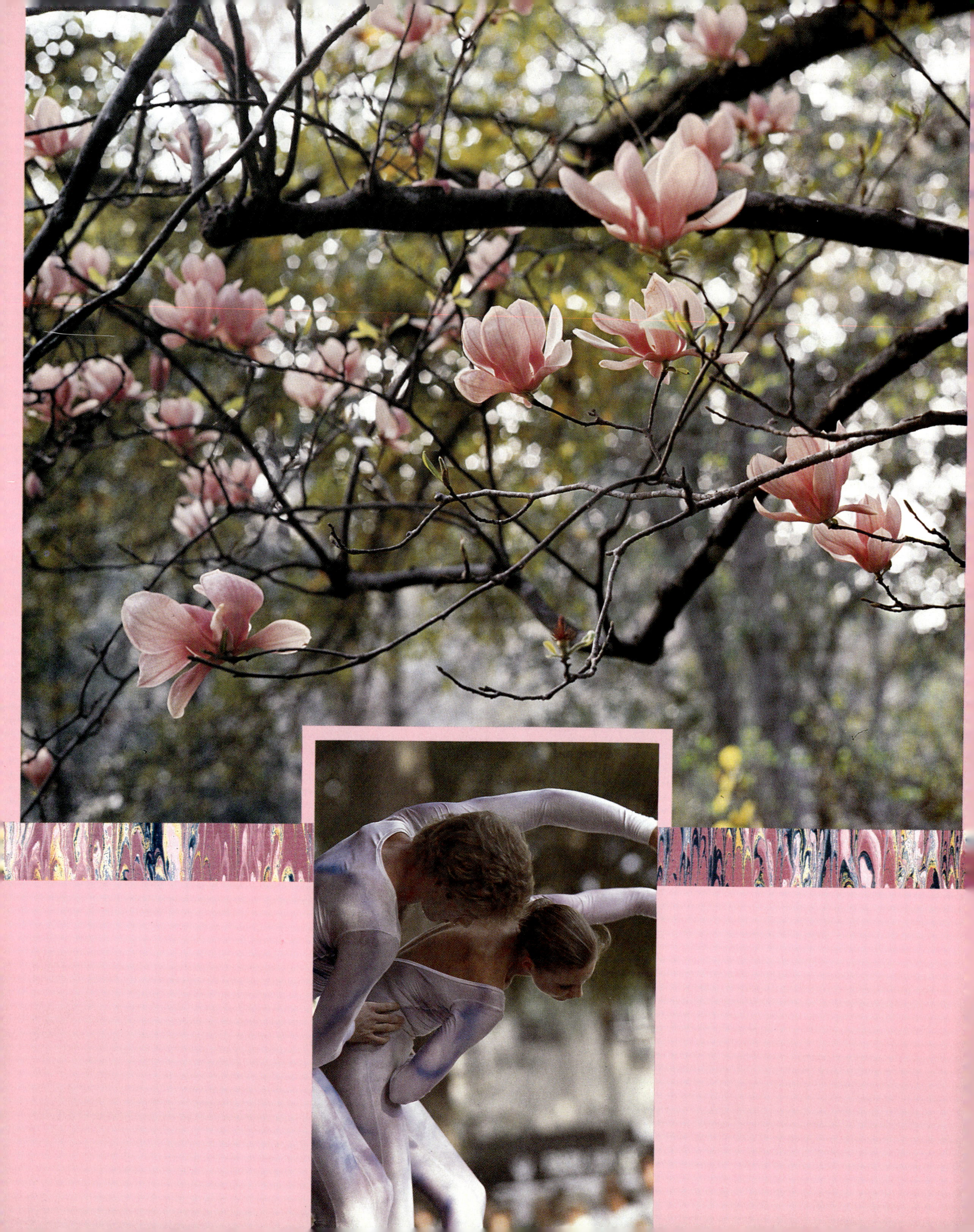

Ornamental magnolias bloom at Leu Gardens. Southern Ballet Theatre performs at the Winter Park Sidewalk Art Festival. Always held the third weekend in March, it is the most prestigious festival of its kind in the Southeast.

Nationally renowned artists display their work at Winter Park Sidewalk Art Festival. □ Mt. Dora Art Festival is held on the sidewalks of Mt. Dora. The city's historic charm and the variety of entertainment have made it one of the most popular art shows in Florida.

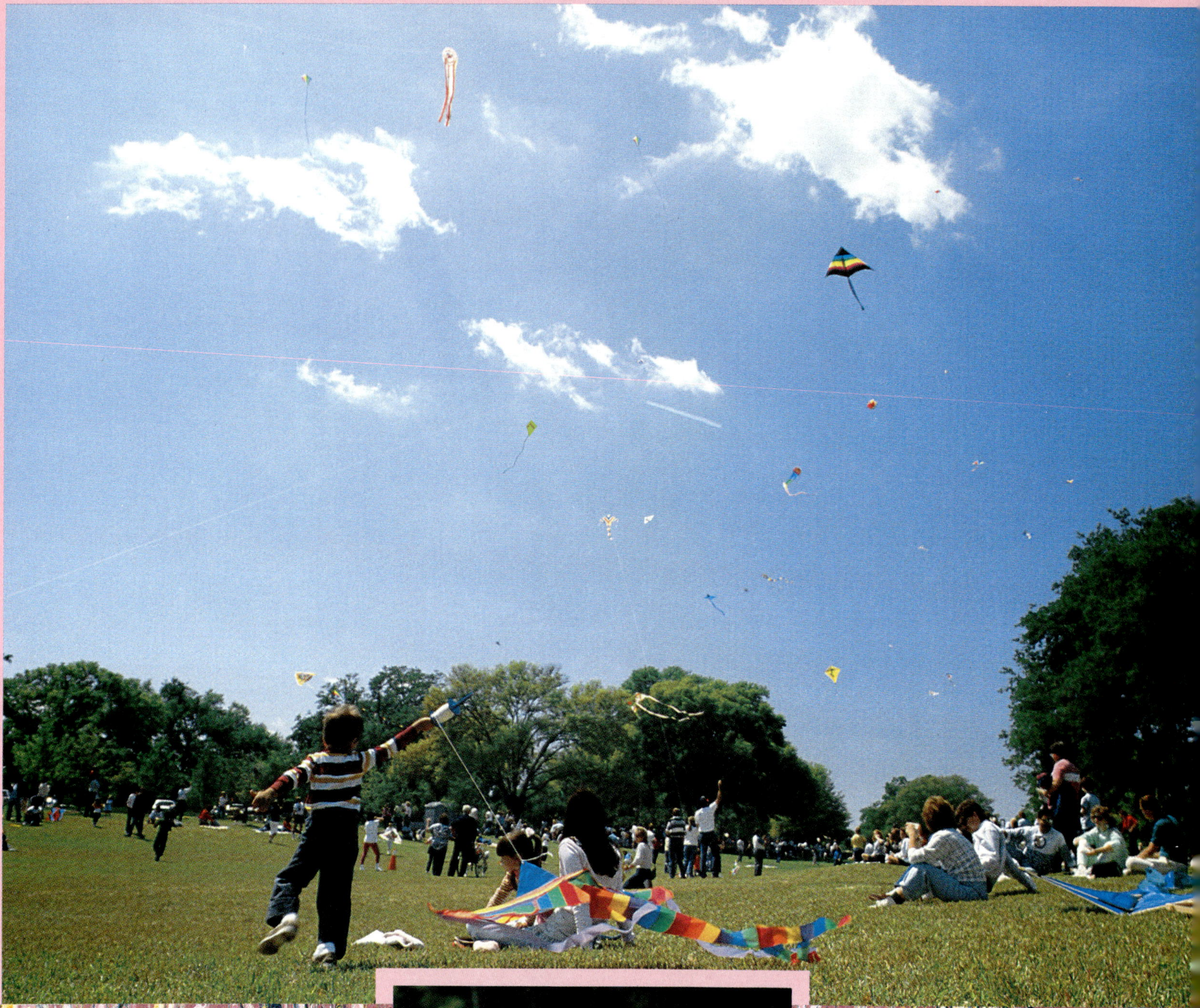

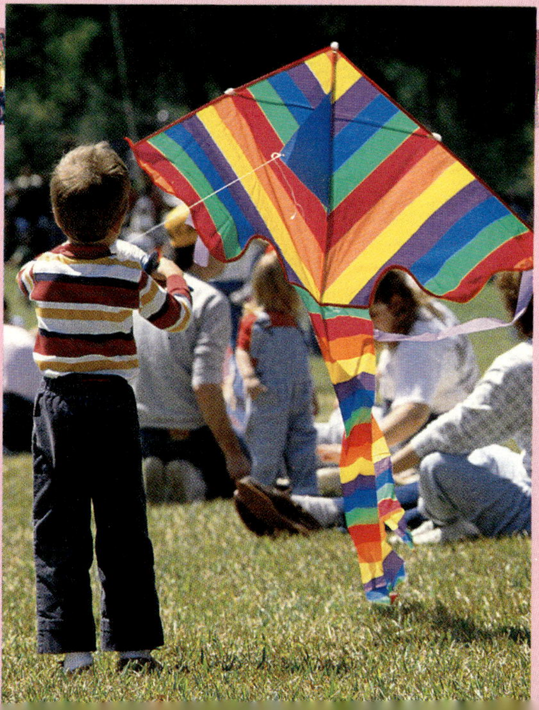

Kite enthusiasts tap March breezes at the annual Kite Festival at Loch Haven Park, near downtown Orlando. Food, entertainment and prizes make for an eventful day.

Orlando Scottish Highland Games at the Central Florida Fairgrounds. □ Orlando celebrates Arts In April. □ Strawberry Spring Festival in Mead Gardens. □ A festival at Pine Castle Center for the Arts. □ Young performers at Winter Park Autumn Art Festival at Rollins College.

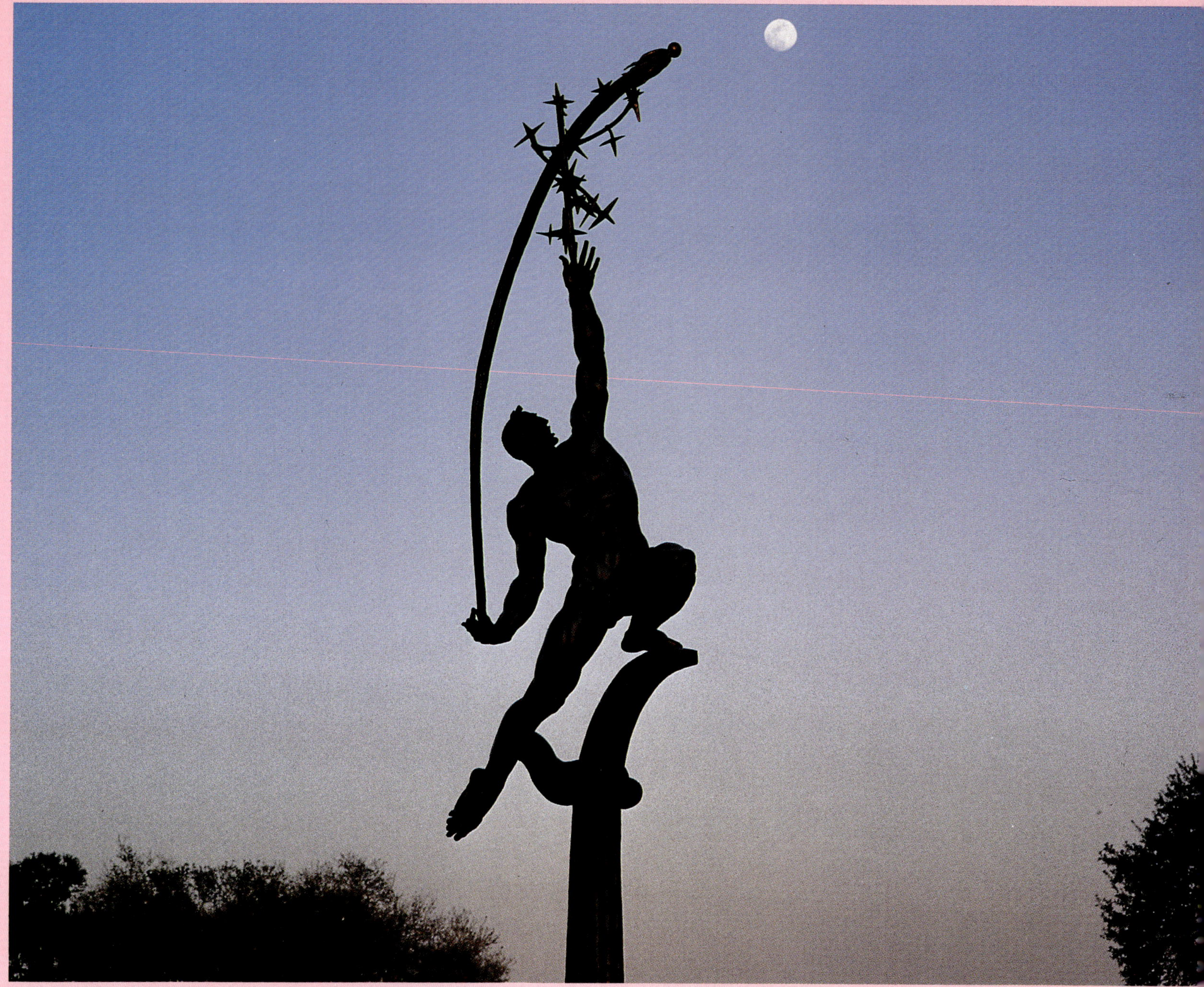

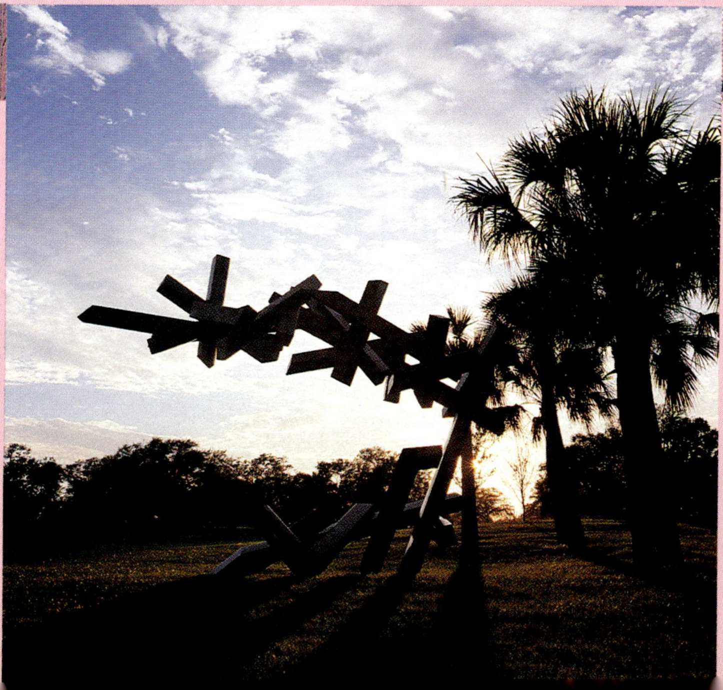

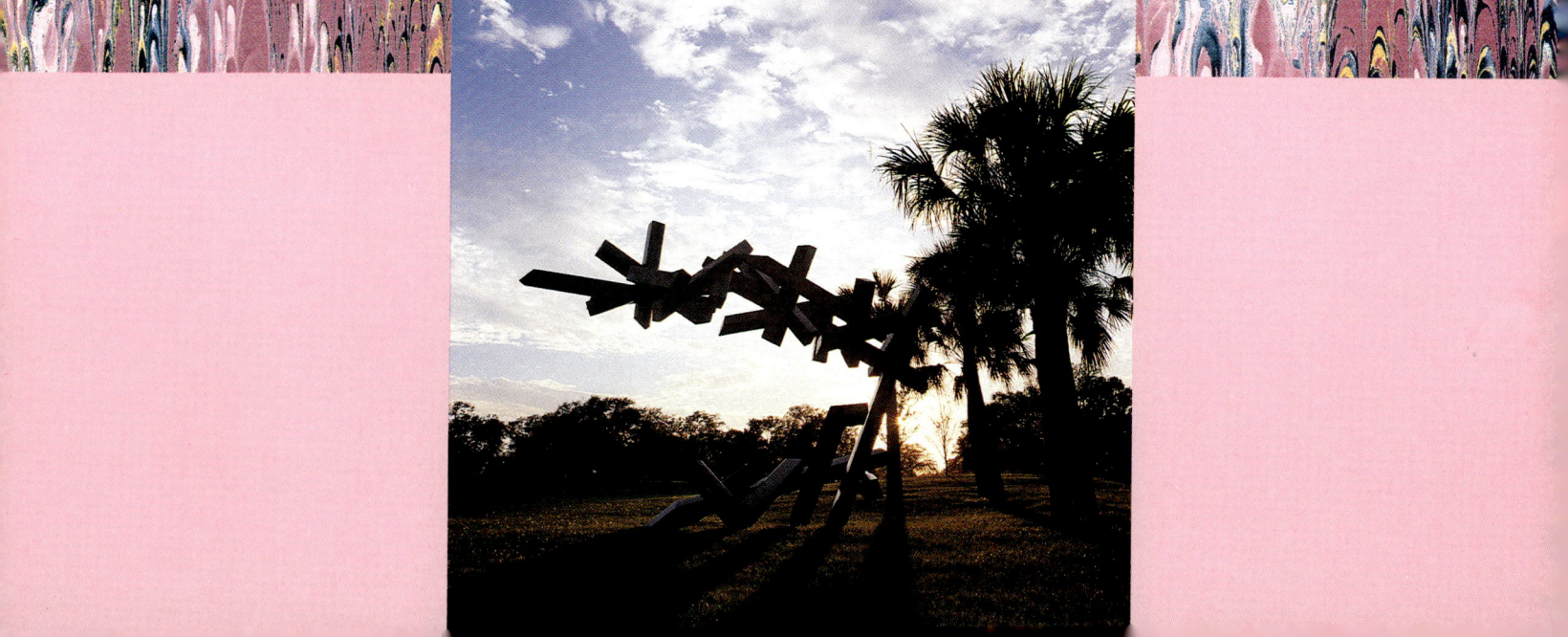

The Rocket Thrower, by Don DeLue, is poised at the entrance to Loch Haven Park. □ Ruins, by Ernest Shaw, sprawls across the lawn in front of the Orlando Museum of Art at Loch Haven.

A frequent spot for school groups, Orlando Science Center in Loch Haven Park offers a hands-on approach with participatory displays, observatory, natural history collection and visiting lecturers. □ School groups also tour Orlando Museum of Art at Loch Haven.

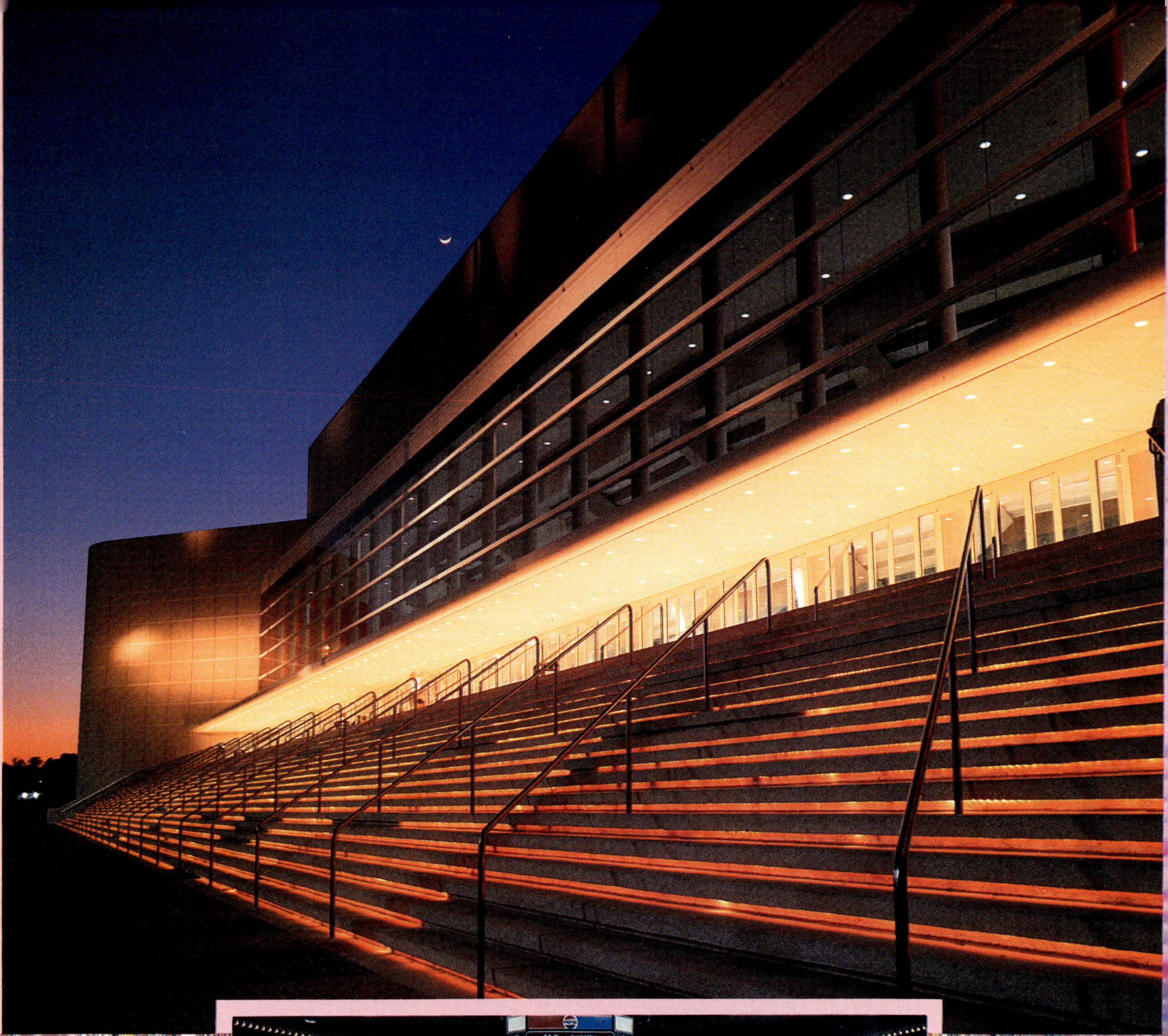

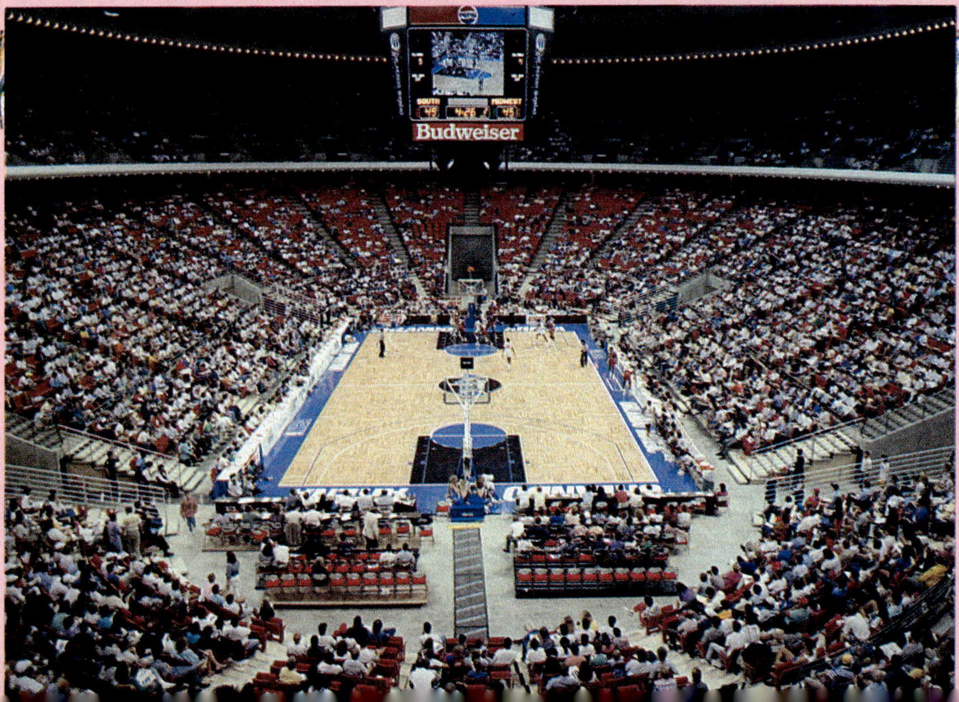
Budweiser

The Orlando Arena rivals big city arenas across the country. More than 15,000 fans make for a capacity crowd at home games. Concerts and other sports events take place in the Arena throughout the year.

The Orlando Magic go head-on with intrastate rivals Miami Heat — and again with the Detroit Pistons. □ The Magic Girls entertain at halftime. □ Stuff, the Magic Dragon, cleans up his act.

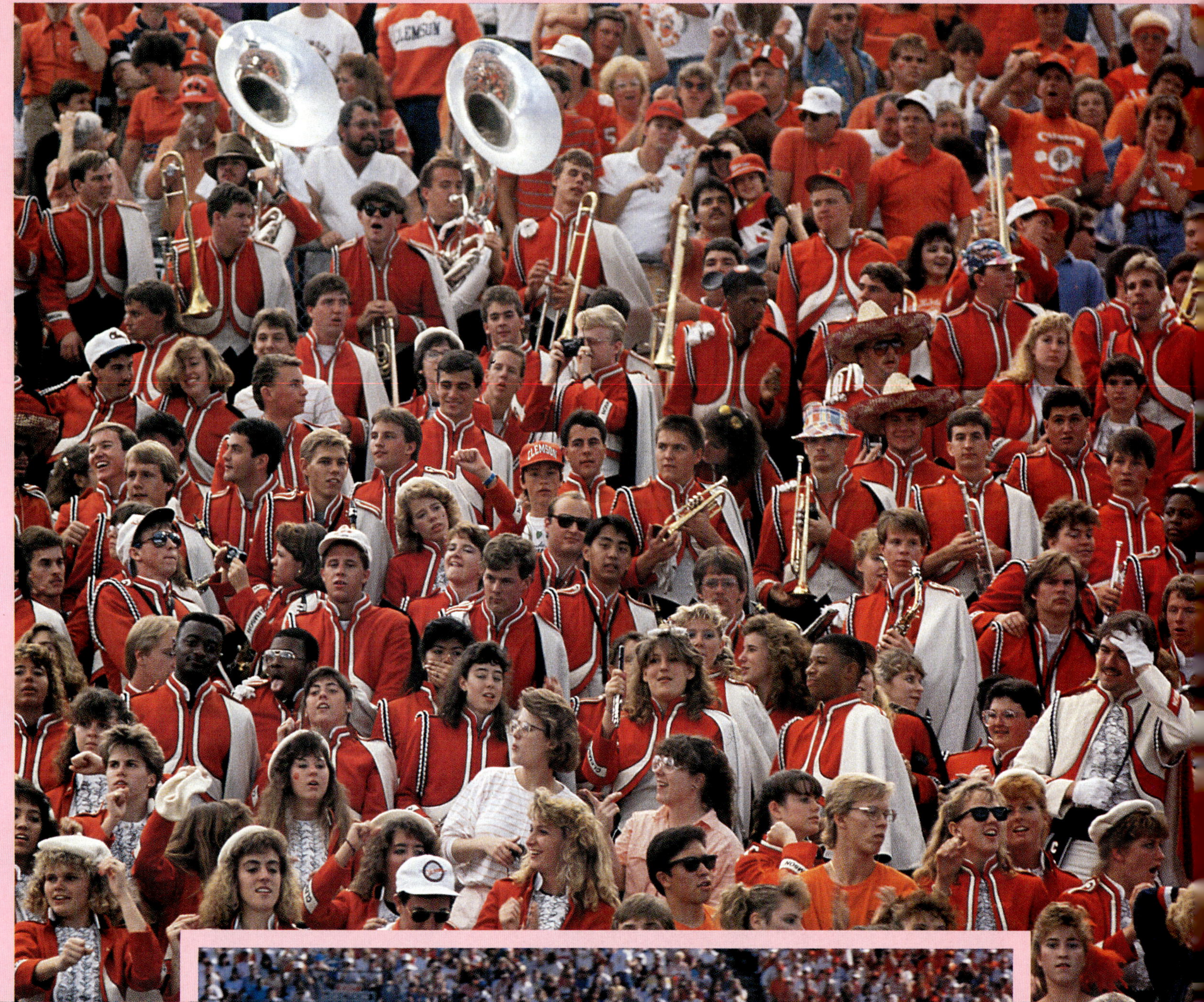
CLEMSON
CLEMSON

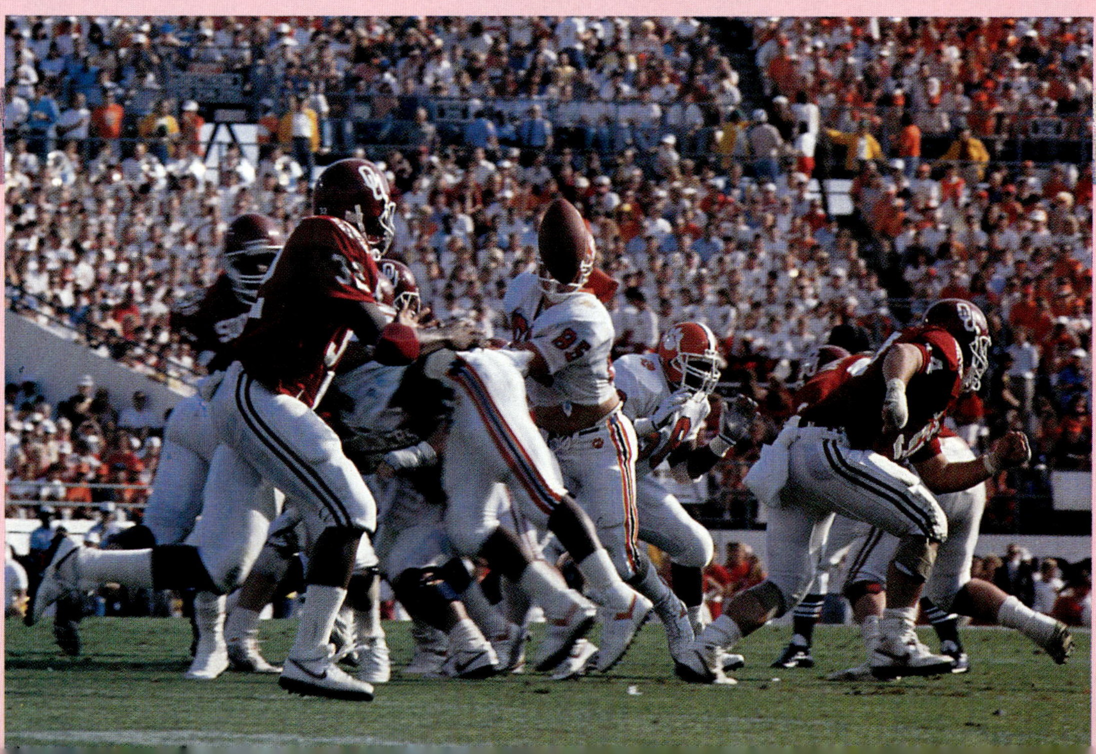

Two nationally ranked college football teams meet at Florida Citrus Bowl-Orlando Stadium for the Florida Citrus Bowl Classic each New Year.

Orlando's sunny skies shine on the fans, pep rallies, half time shows and Florida Citrus Bowl Parade. Network television carries the game and parade to bowl watchers all over the country.

Delta
Court of Flags
McNamara
Pontiac
WE COVER
ALL THE BASES
Prime Steaks
Seafood
740-8282
32

32

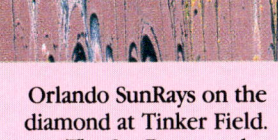

Orlando SunRays on the diamond at Tinker Field. The SunRays are the Minnesota Twins Class AA Southern League franchise.

A major leaguer signs autographs during spring training. □ Fans at Tinker Field. □ Color guard at Baseball City Stadium. Houston Astros play it safe and delight fans during major league spring training.

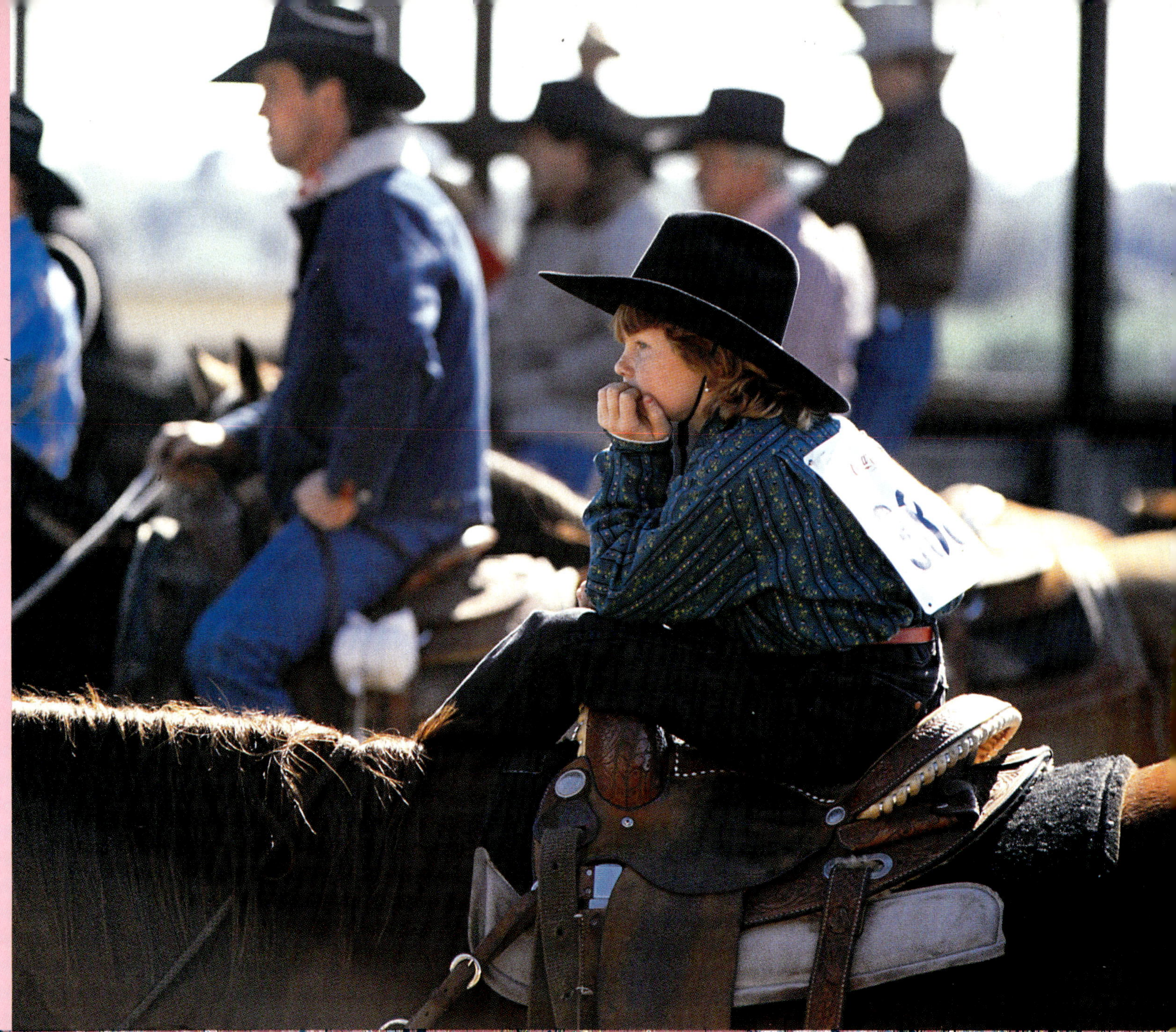

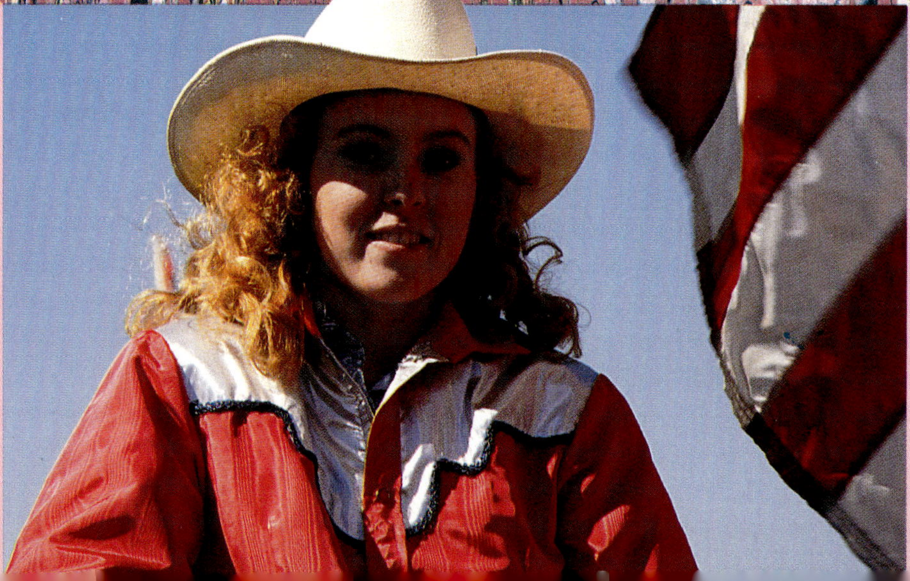

Each February the Silver Spurs Rodeo is held in Kissimmee and draws top professional cowboys from the United States and Canada — and lots of spectators.

Silver Spurs is one of the oldest and largest professional rodeos in the South. Prize money is earned in steer roping and riding events held over the four day celebration.

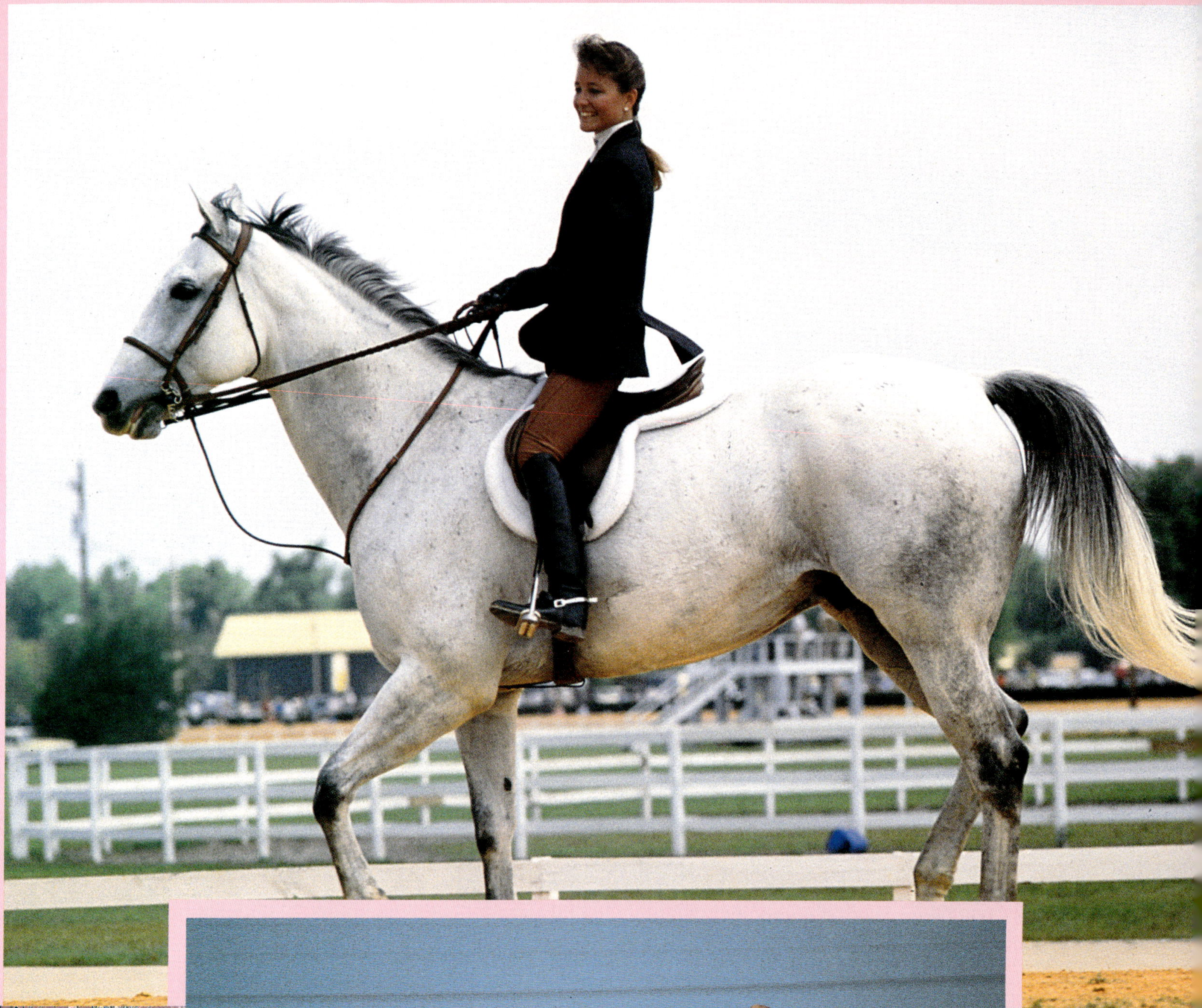

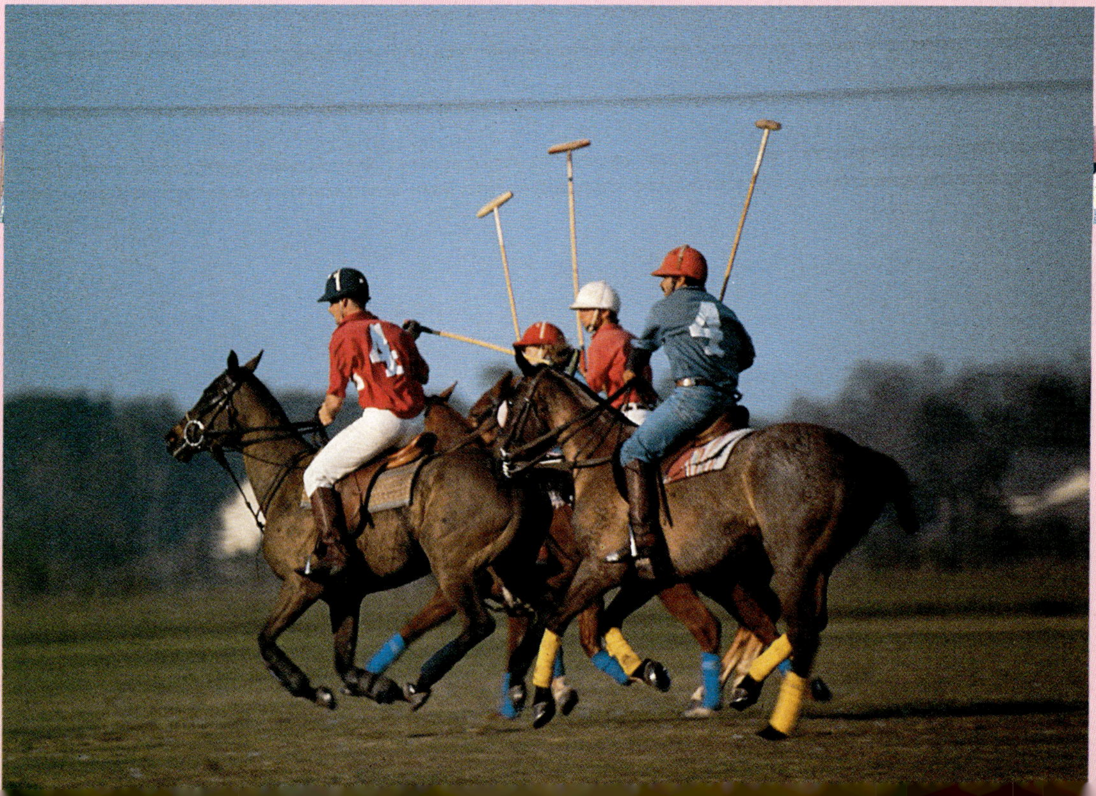

The Marshal leads the post parade for the sulky races at Ben White Raceway. The sport of kings is played at Lee Vista Center, near Orlando International Airport.

Windsurfing and all kinds of boating are a natural on Lake Underhill. □ Lake Ivanhoe plays host to many amateur and professional ski tournaments. □ Orlando Lions bring professional soccer to Orlando. Golden South Classic hosts top high school track and field athletes at Showalter Field in Winter Park.

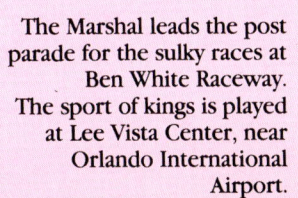

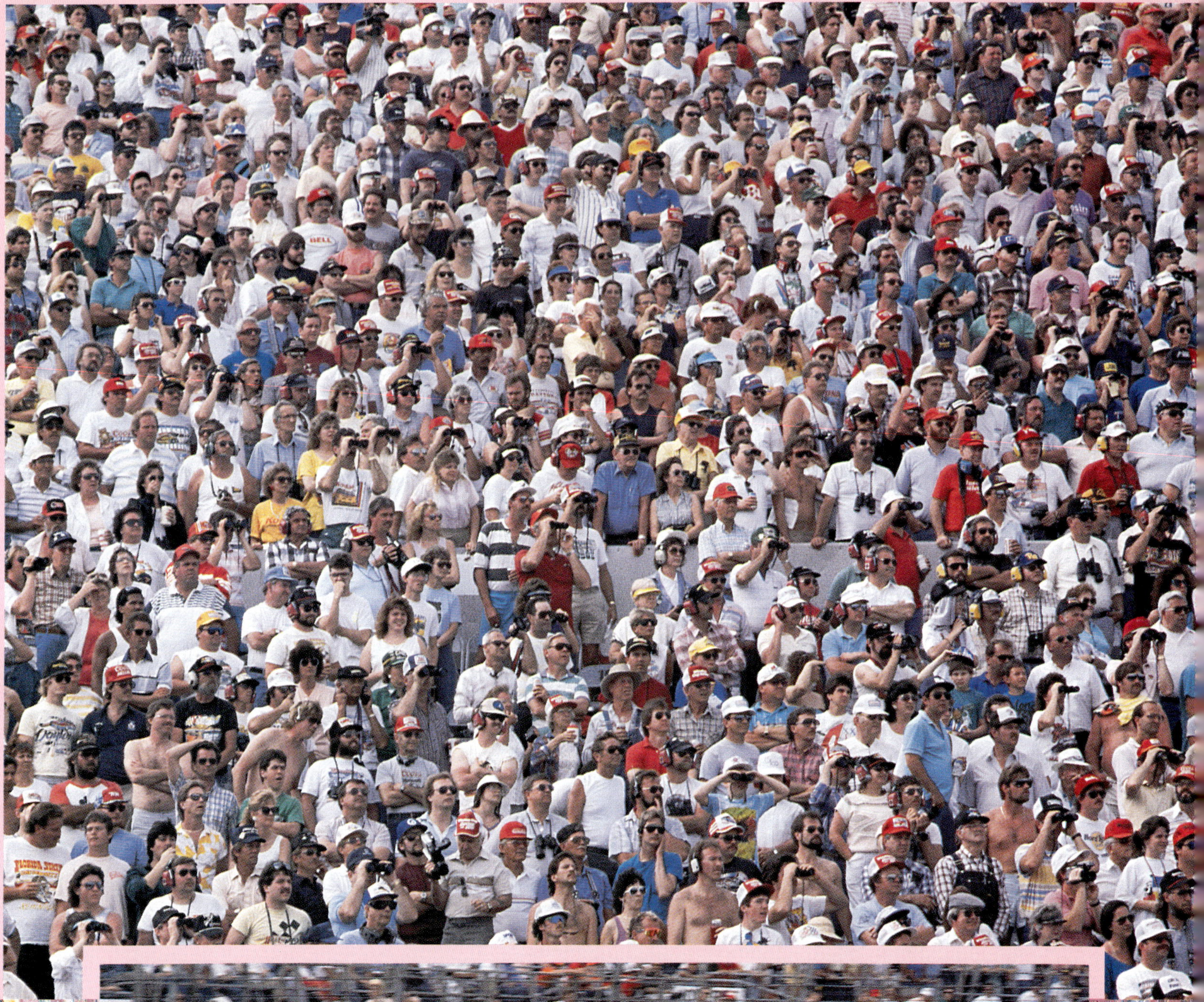

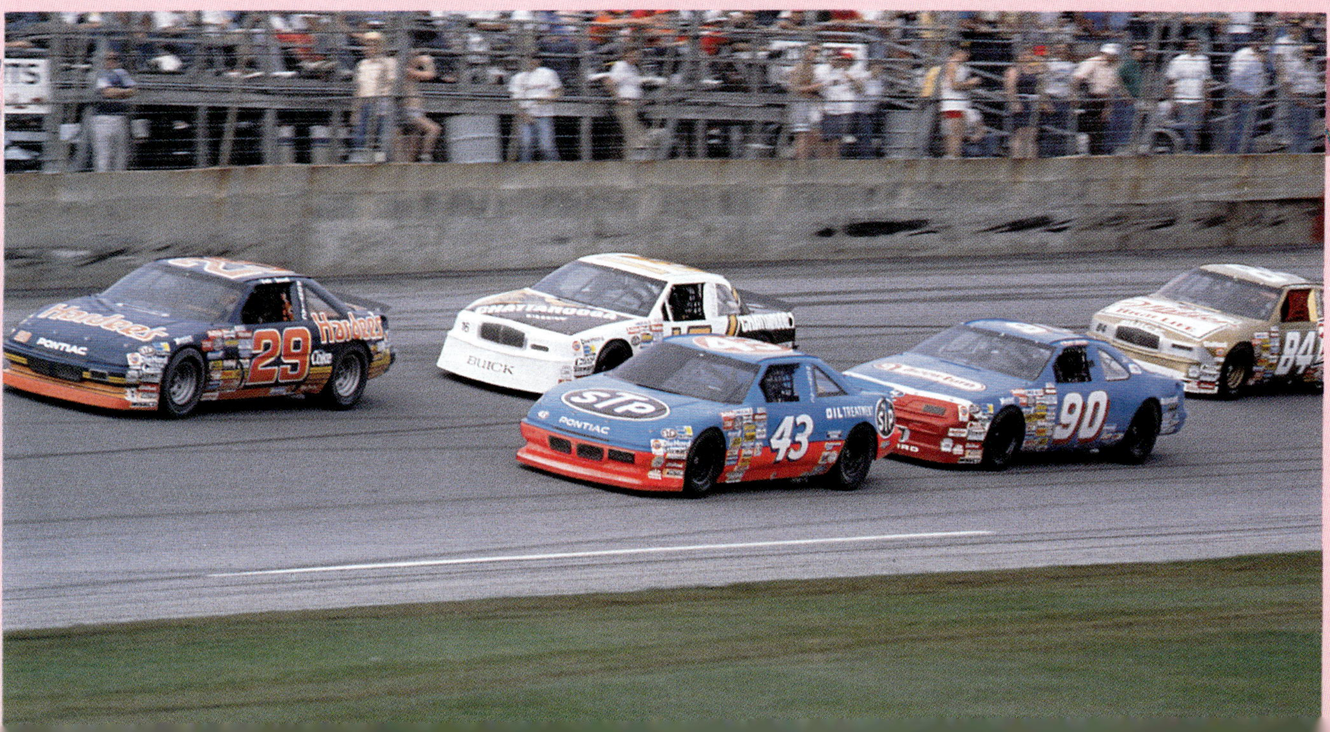
29
STP
PONTIAC
43
90
84
BUICK

Daytona International Speedway hosts hundreds of thousands of race fans who turn out — and millions who tune in on national television — for such NASCAR favorites as the Firecracker 400 and Daytona 500.

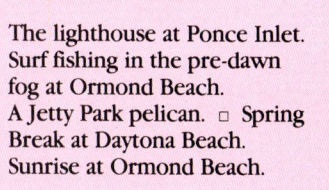

The lighthouse at Ponce Inlet. Surf fishing in the pre-dawn fog at Ormond Beach. A Jetty Park pelican. □ Spring Break at Daytona Beach. Sunrise at Ormond Beach.

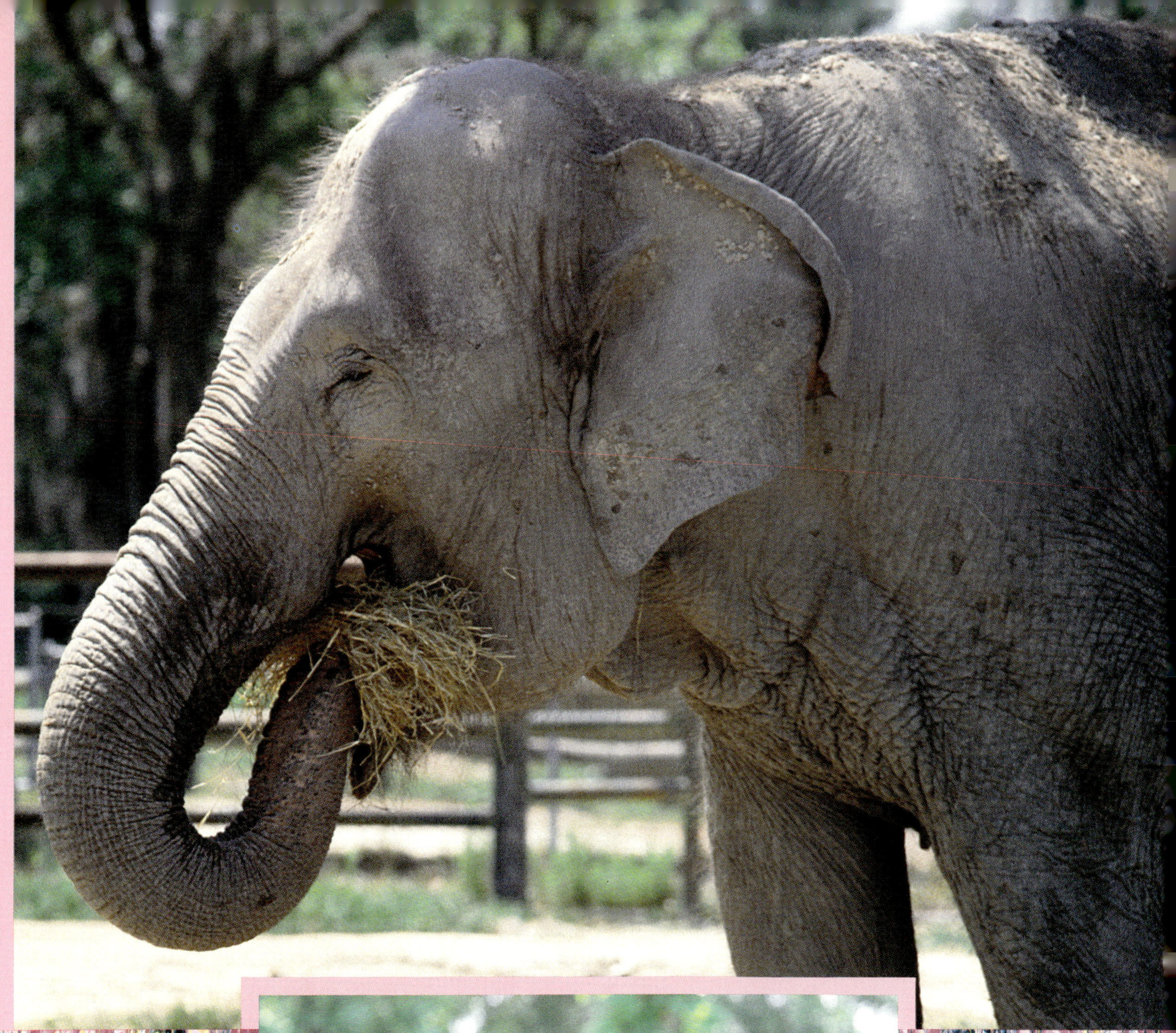

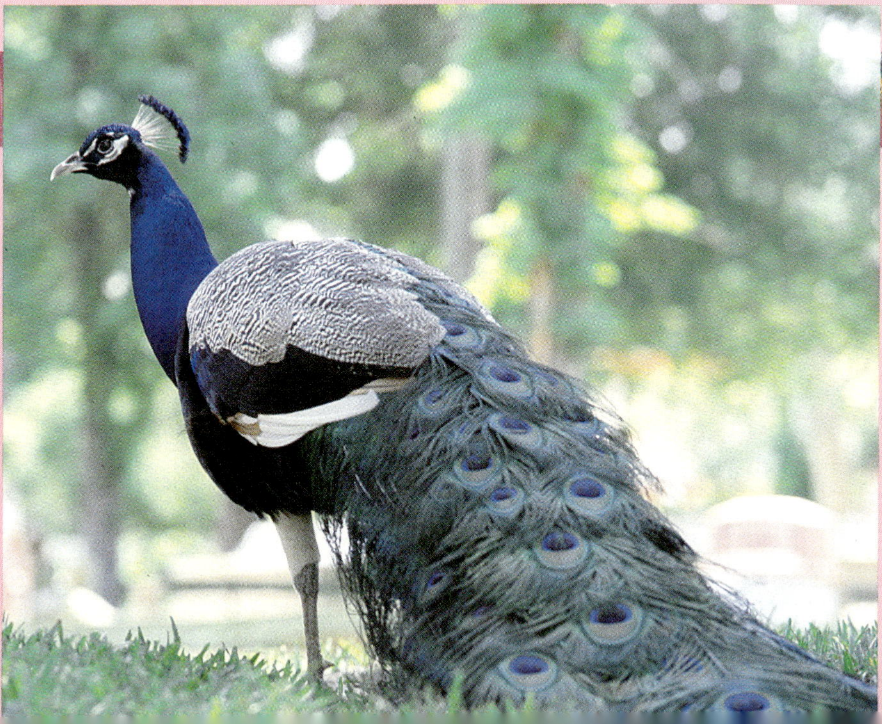

The 110-acre Central Florida Zoo is popular with residents and tourists alike. It features more than 400 native and exotic animals in a setting that's truly Florida.

Some notable residents: Asian elephants, peacocks, black leopards, Bengal tiger, North American river otters, American crocodiles and ostriches.

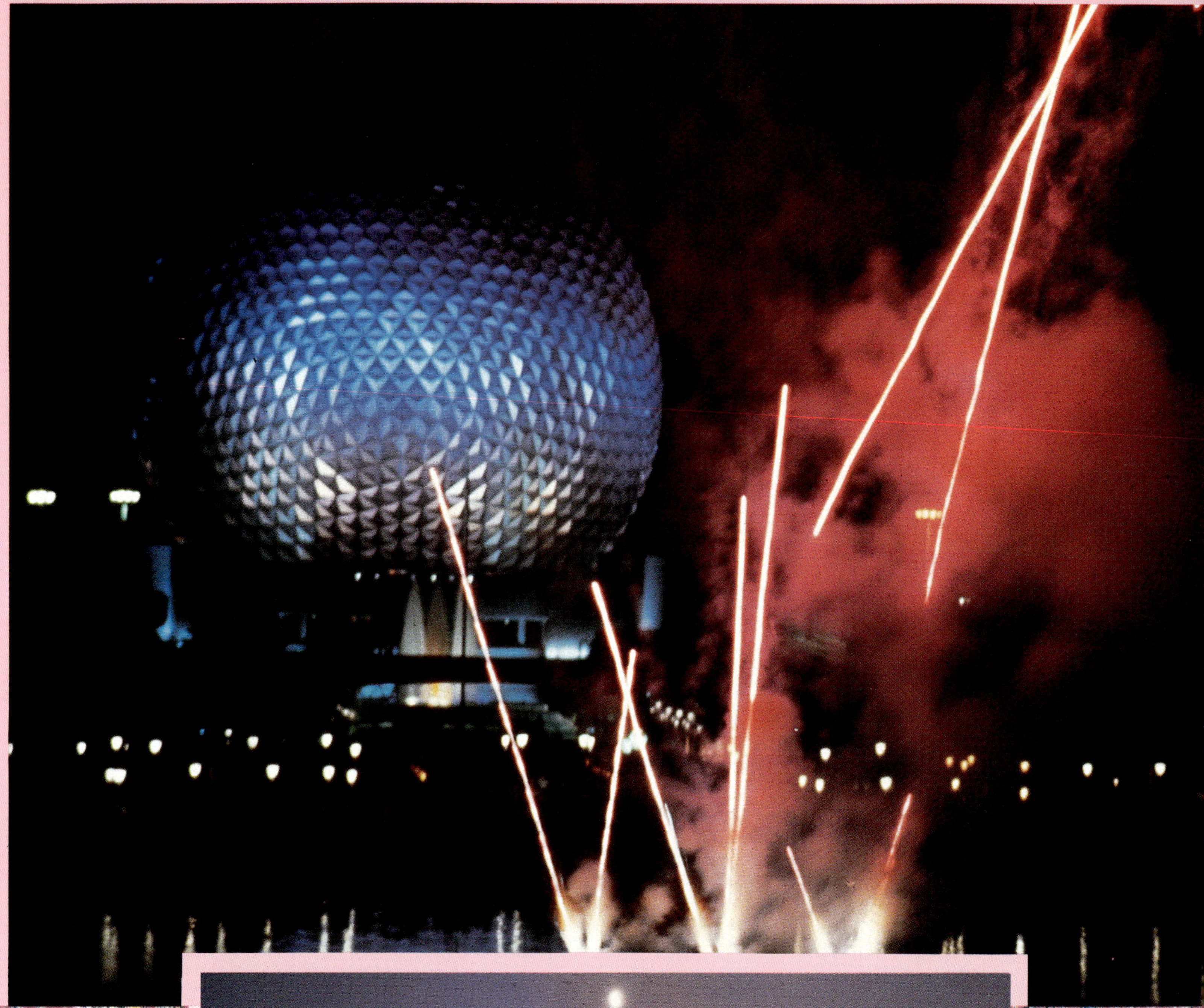

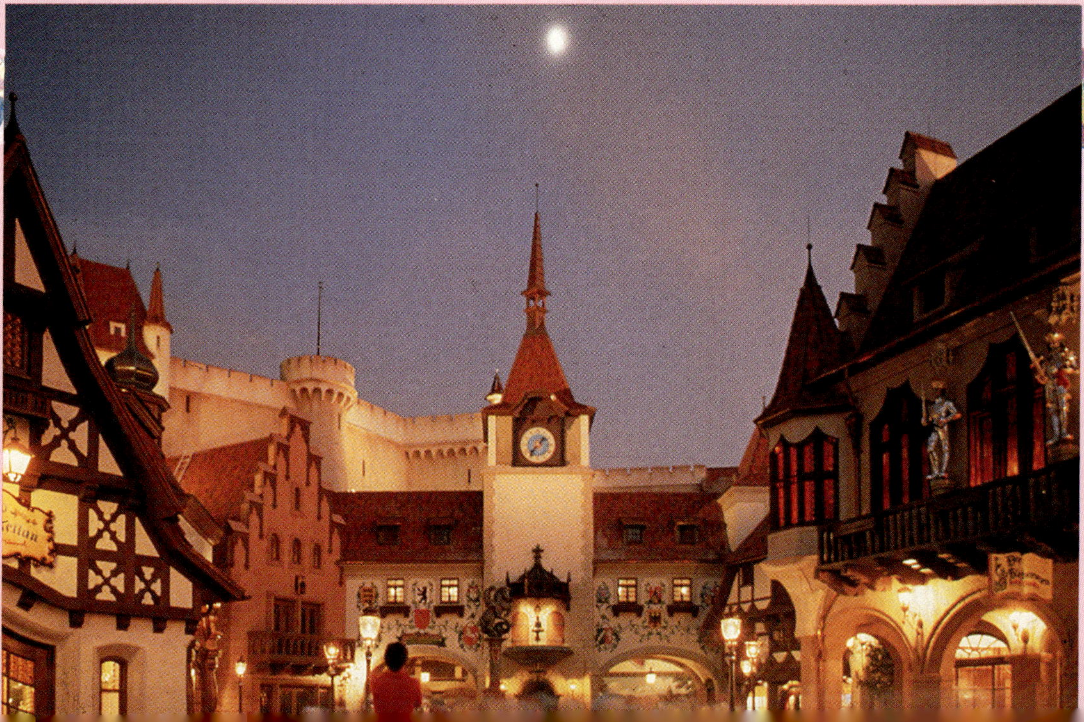

The laser light show, IllumiNations, is a special effects extravaganza across World Showcase Lagoon nightly at Epcot Center. Visitors tour Germany at World Showcase.

The view from Main Street of fireworks over Cinderella's Castle. ☐ Riding Thunder Mountain. Mickey Mouse snorkels through The Living Seas and motors through Mickey's Birthdayland.

Photos courtesy of Walt Disney World©

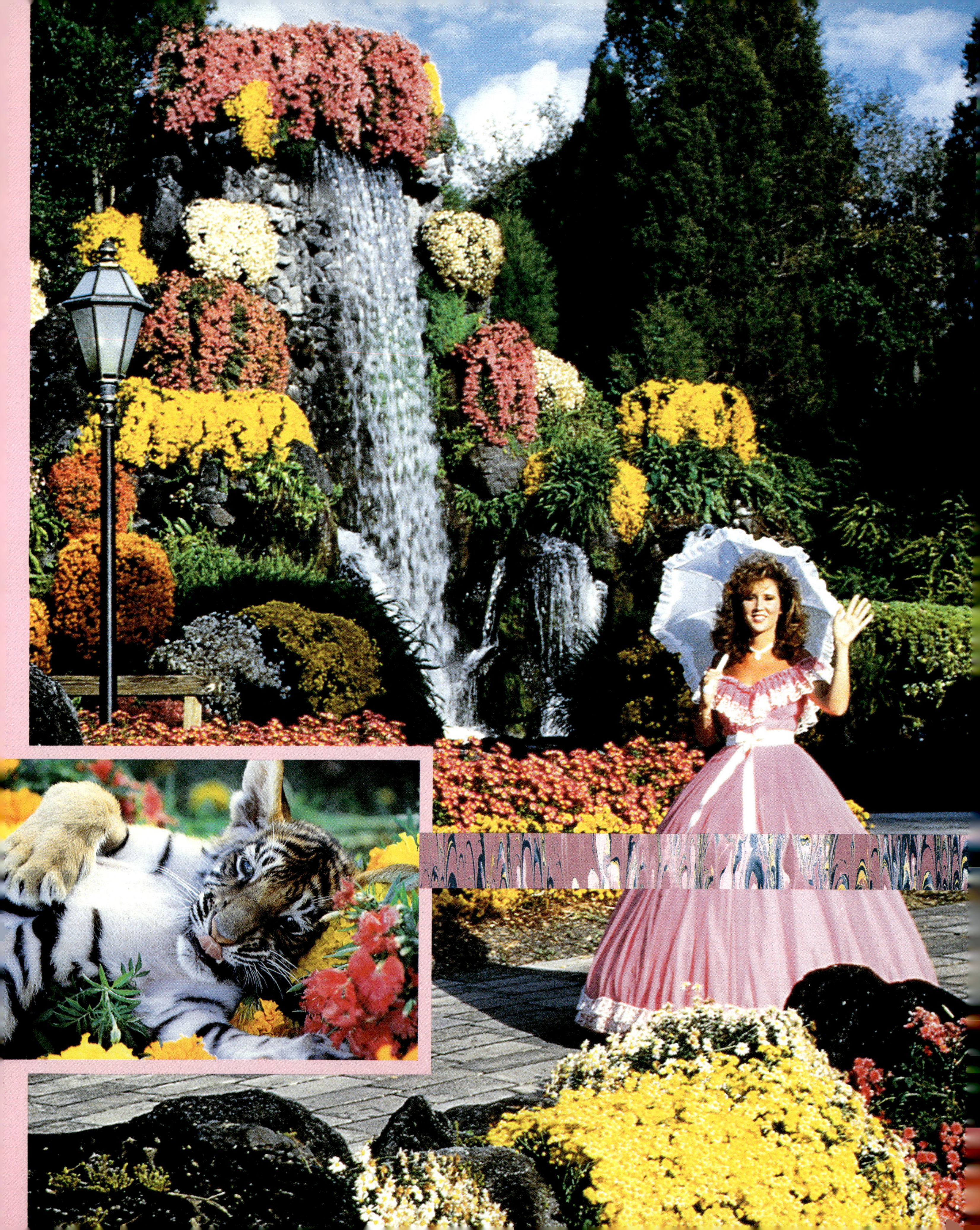

Chrysanthemums on parade at Cypress Gardens in Winter Haven. A baby tiger rests among some of the 8,000 varieties of flowers at Cypress Gardens, Florida's oldest tourist attraction. At Sea World: flamingos in the World of the Sea Lagoon; Shamu's antics in Shamu Stadium; sea lion and otter show, with special walrus guest star; Atlantic bottle nose dolphins; macaws; and beluga whales.

Photos courtesy Cypress Gardens© and SeaWorld©

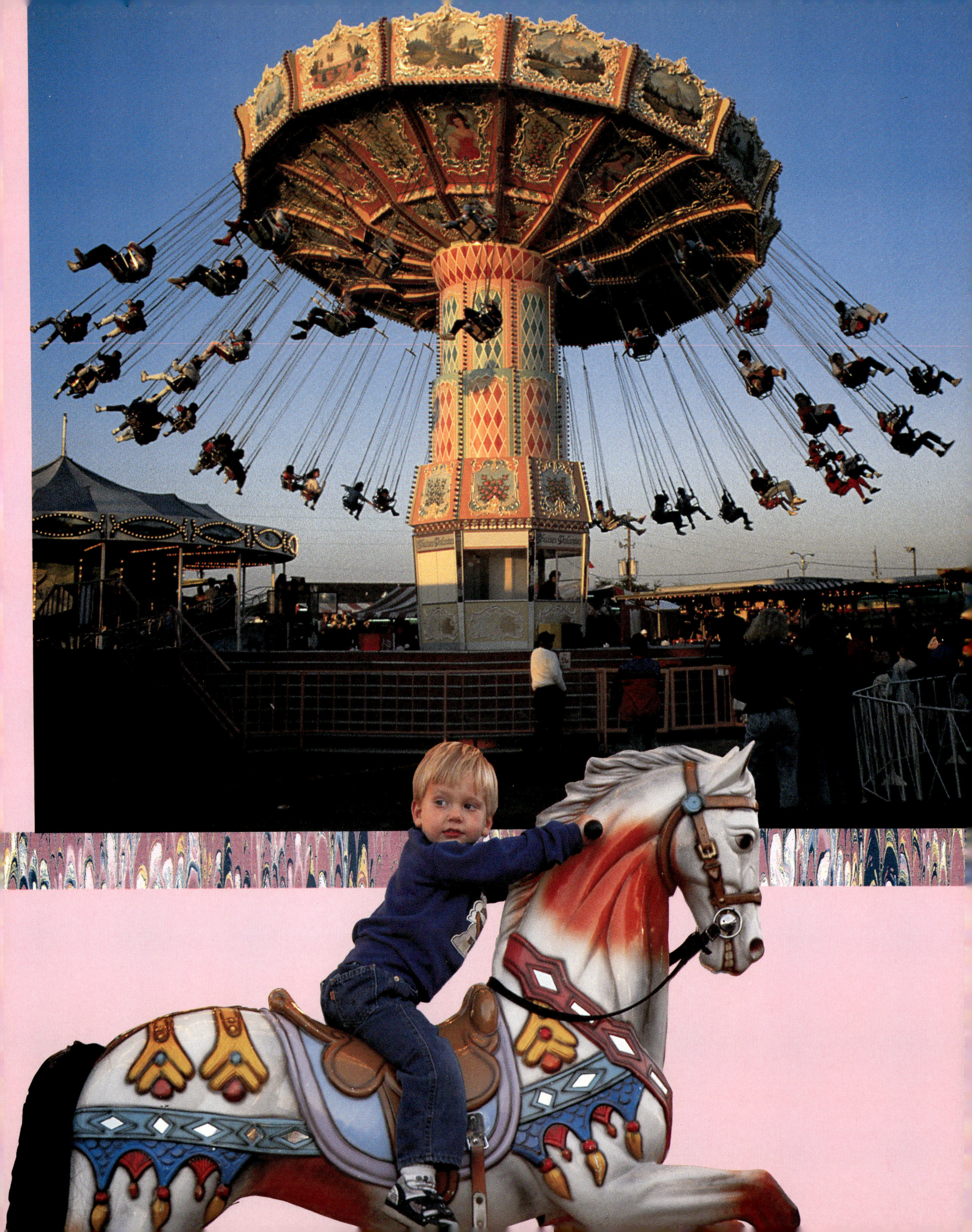

The Central Florida Fair brings midways, James E. Strates Shows, livestock exhibits, and national entertainment each March.

Dusk creates even more atmosphere on Hollywood Boulevard at Universal Studios Florida. A live stunt show explodes with excitement at the lagoon. A classic car in front of Mel's American Graffiti Drive-In. ☐ The Hard Rock Cafe lights up the night.

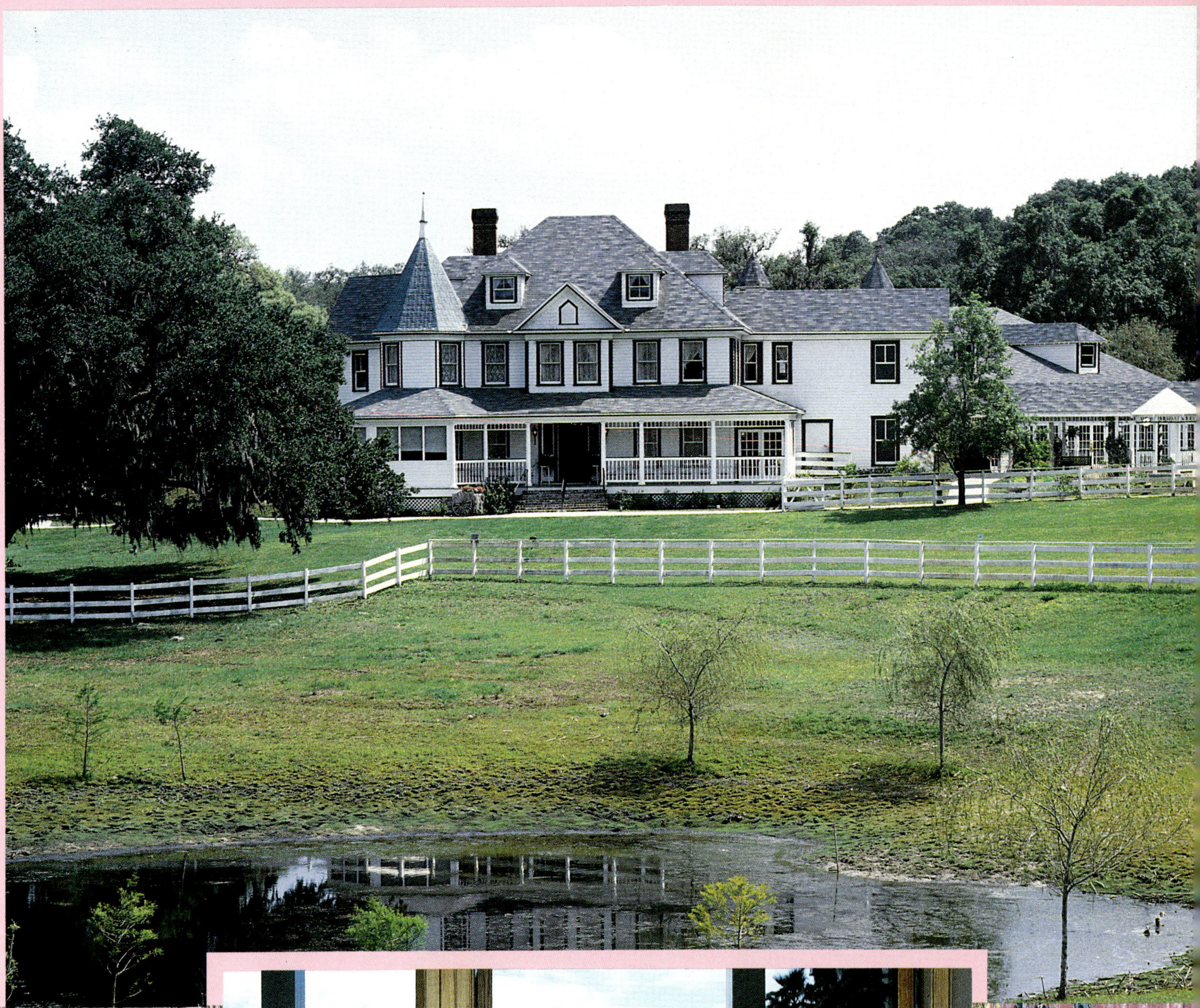

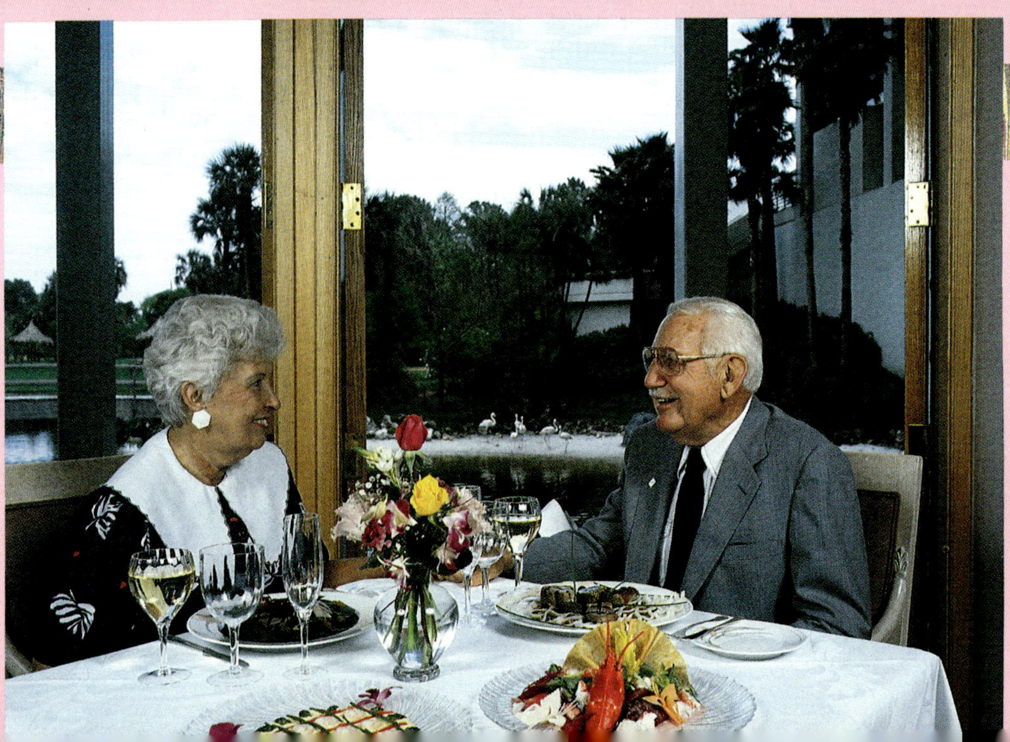

Restored in Norman Rockwell style, Townsend's Plantation in Apopka serves traditional Southern cooking. La Coquina, at Hyatt Regency Grand Cypress, is noted for its elegant gourmet cuisine.

The Olive Garden has several locations in Central Florida. A cafe on Church Street. Bailey's Cityside on Church Street. ☐ Vivaldi serves Italian fare on Pine Street. Hemingways, at Hyatt Regency Grand Cypress, has the look of Key West.

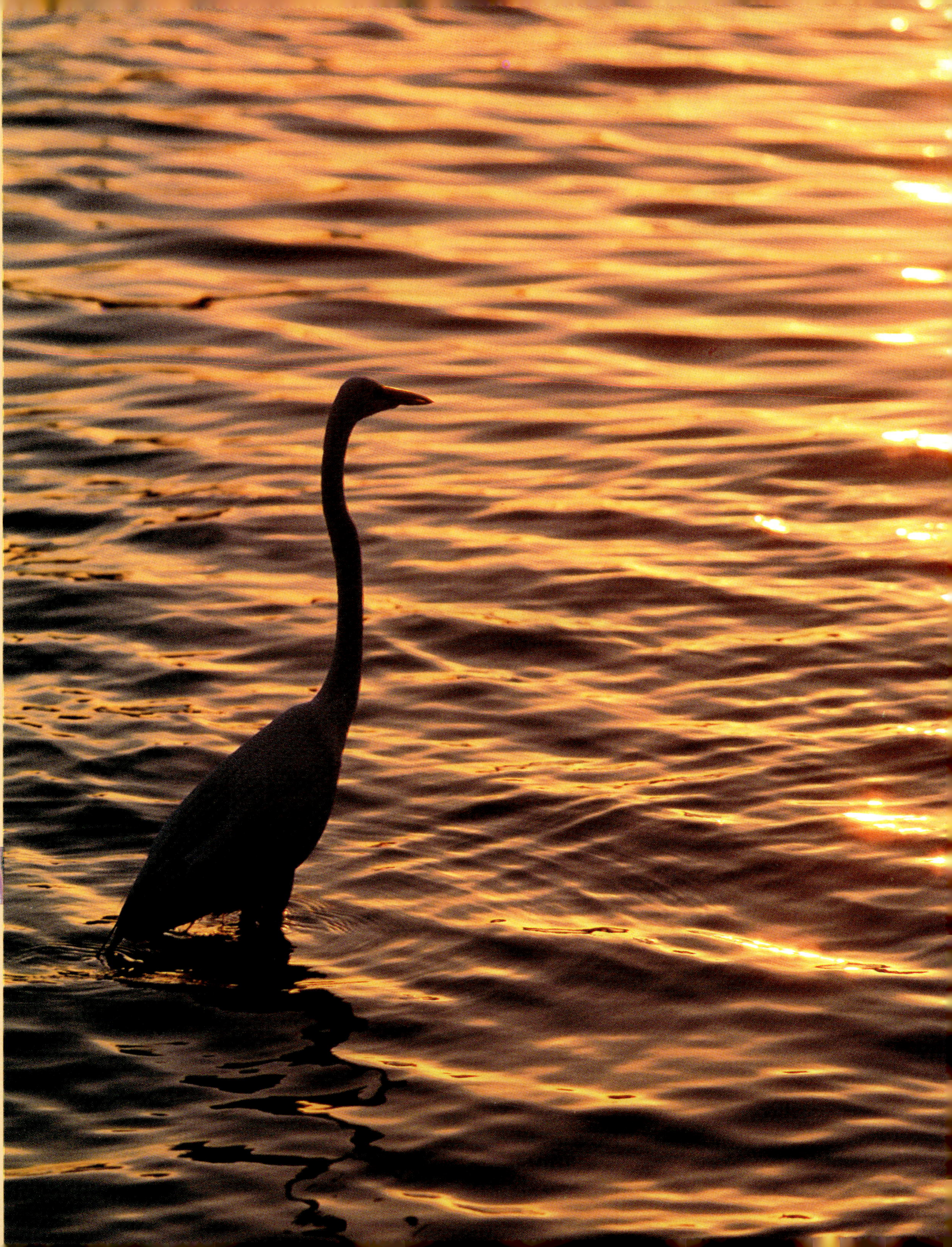

All Things Bright And Beautiful

Open spaces, wildlife, natural beauty. Orlando has an abundance of all of these.

The landscape is speckled with hundreds of lakes and freshwater springs, providing a rich habitat for native wildlife. Well cared for parks are here by the dozens — from the heart of downtown to outlying rural areas.

So turn the page for a look at Orlando's bright and beautiful world.

A heron witnesses sunset from the shores of Lake Eola.

A field of phlox welcomes Spring.

A bald eagle at Florida Audubon Society's Center for Birds of Prey.

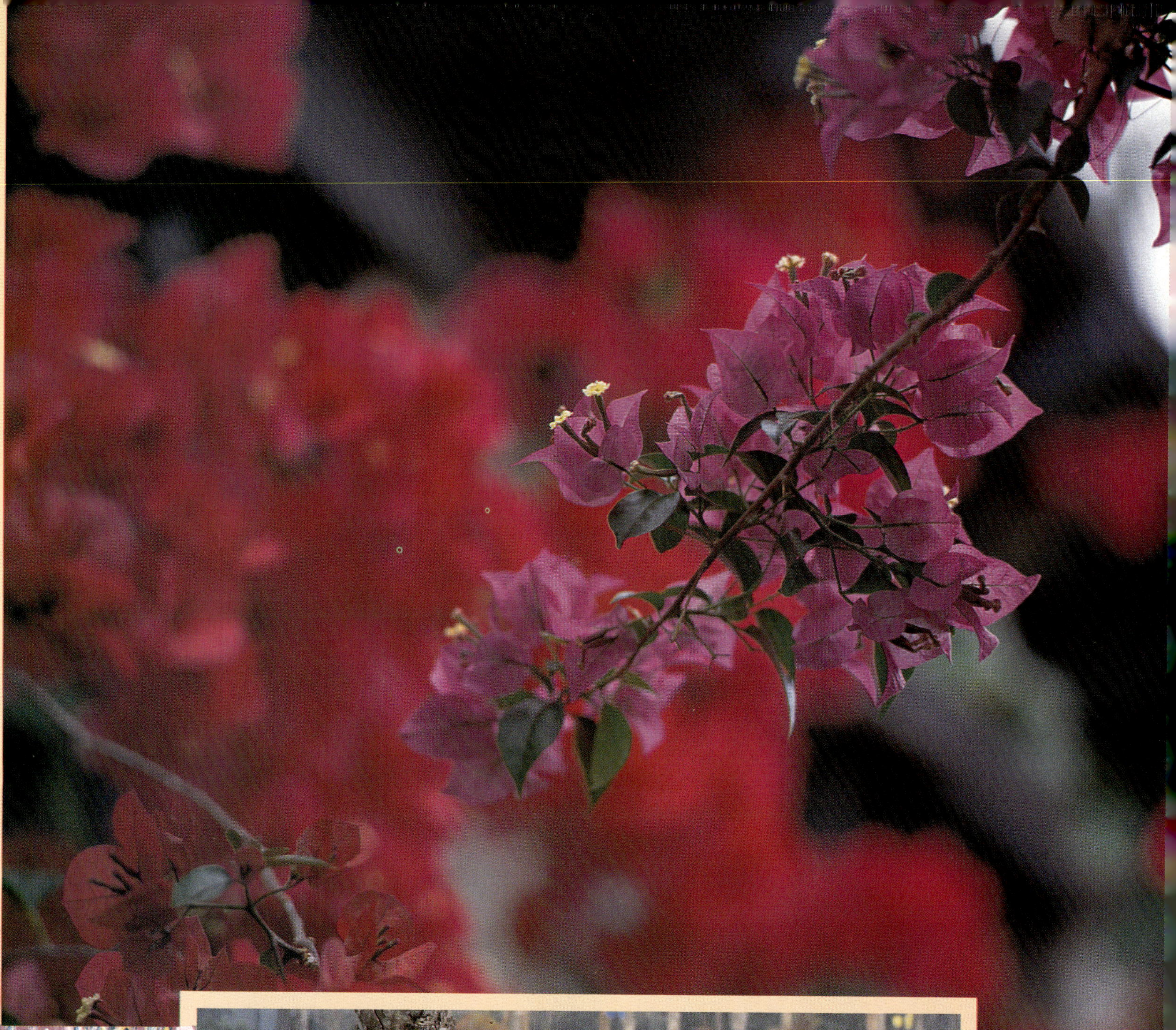

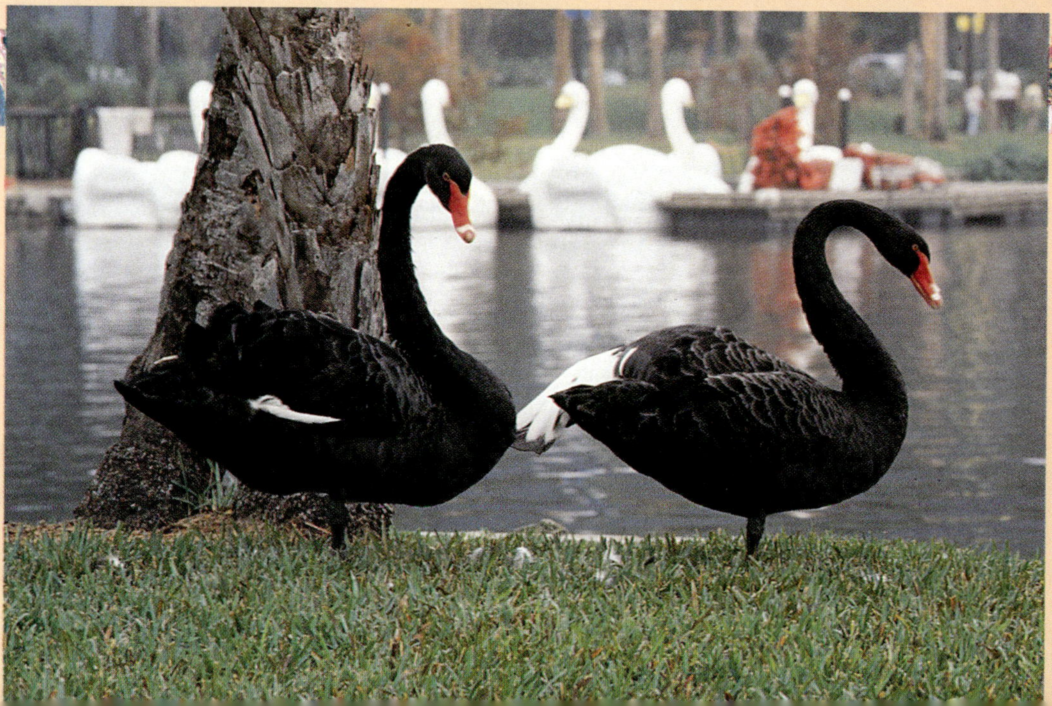

Nature paints a colorful canvas in the courtyard of the Maitland Art Center. □ A pair of black swans take in the sights around Lake Eola in the heart of downtown.

Leu Gardens, in Orlando near Winter Park, has 57 acres of botanical gardens and a historic turn-of-the-century Florida home. □ Eola Park is noted for its fountain in the center of Lake Eola. □ A shaded walkway in Leu Gardens.

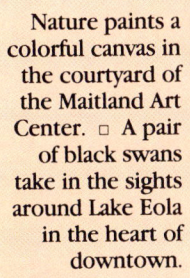

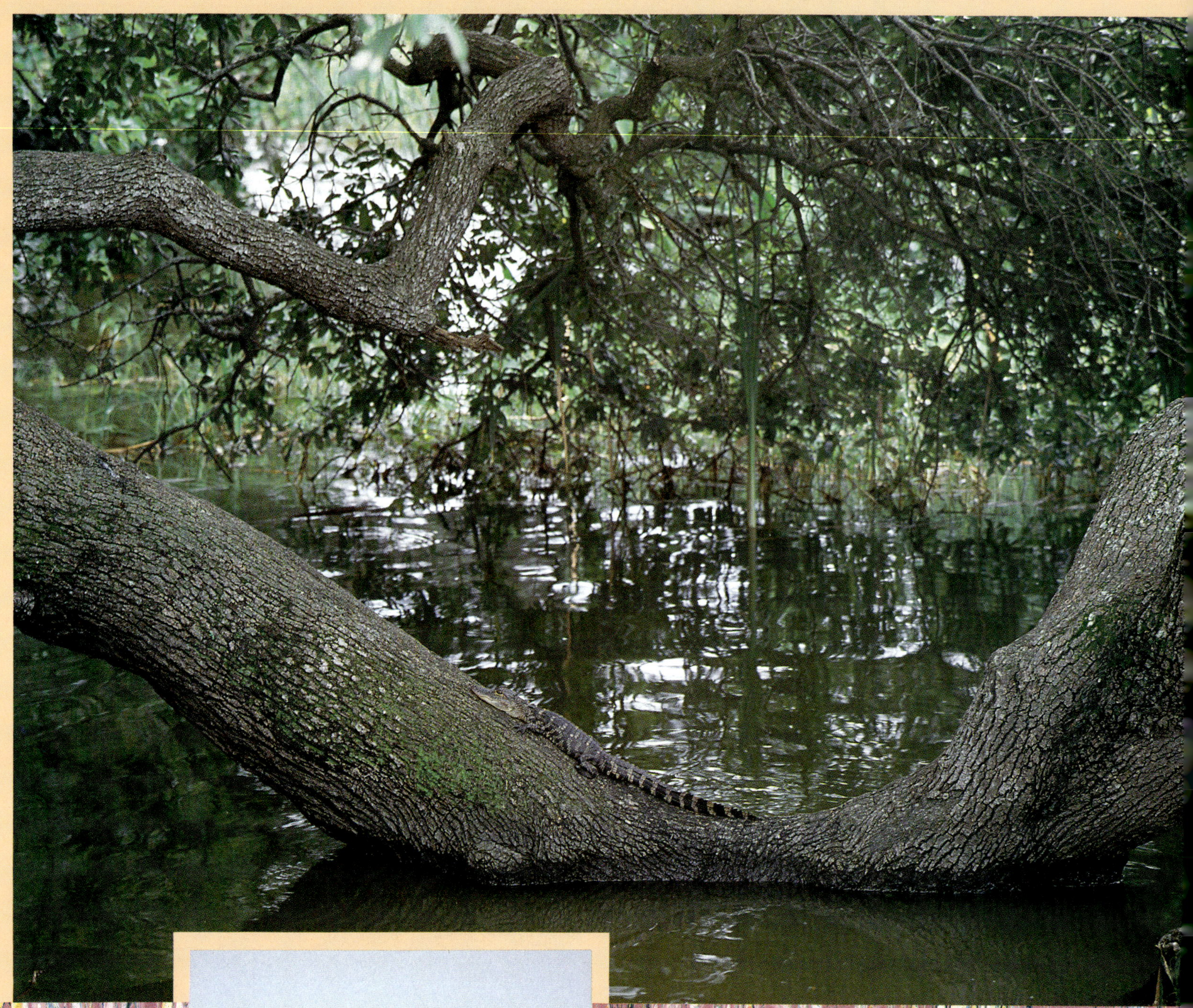
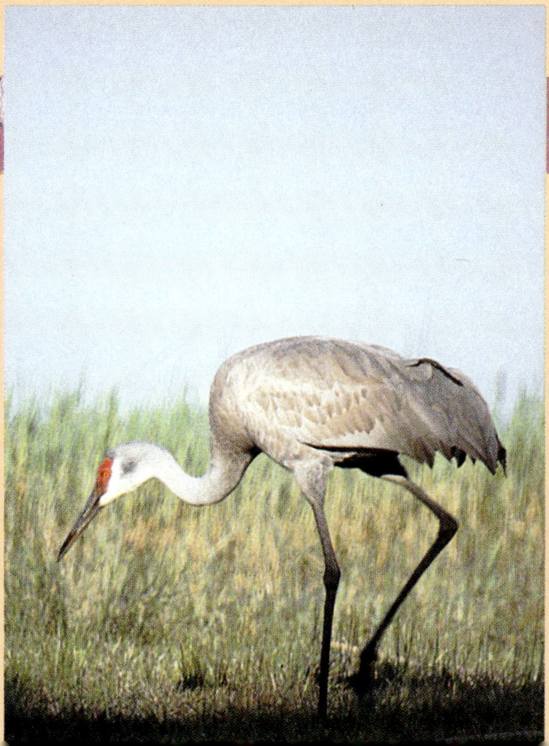
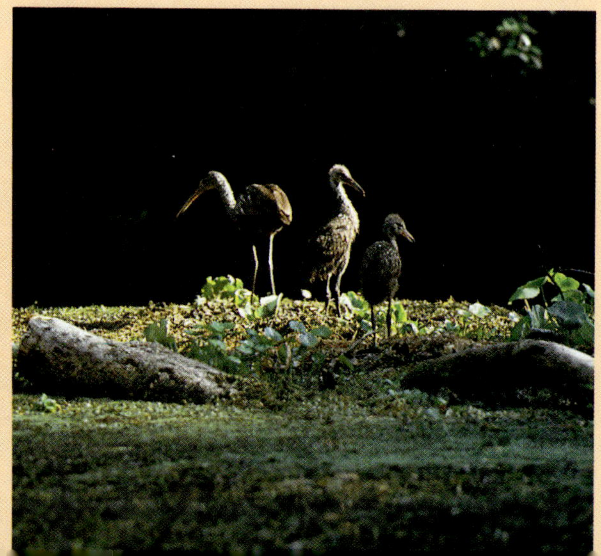

A baby alligator catches some rays at Lake Dora. A sand hill crane in Moss Park. Young limpkins thrive on the Wekiva River.

Sunset on Lake Dora. □ Late afternoon on Deseret Ranch in southeast Orange County. □ Morning at Cracker Farm in Turkey Lake Park.

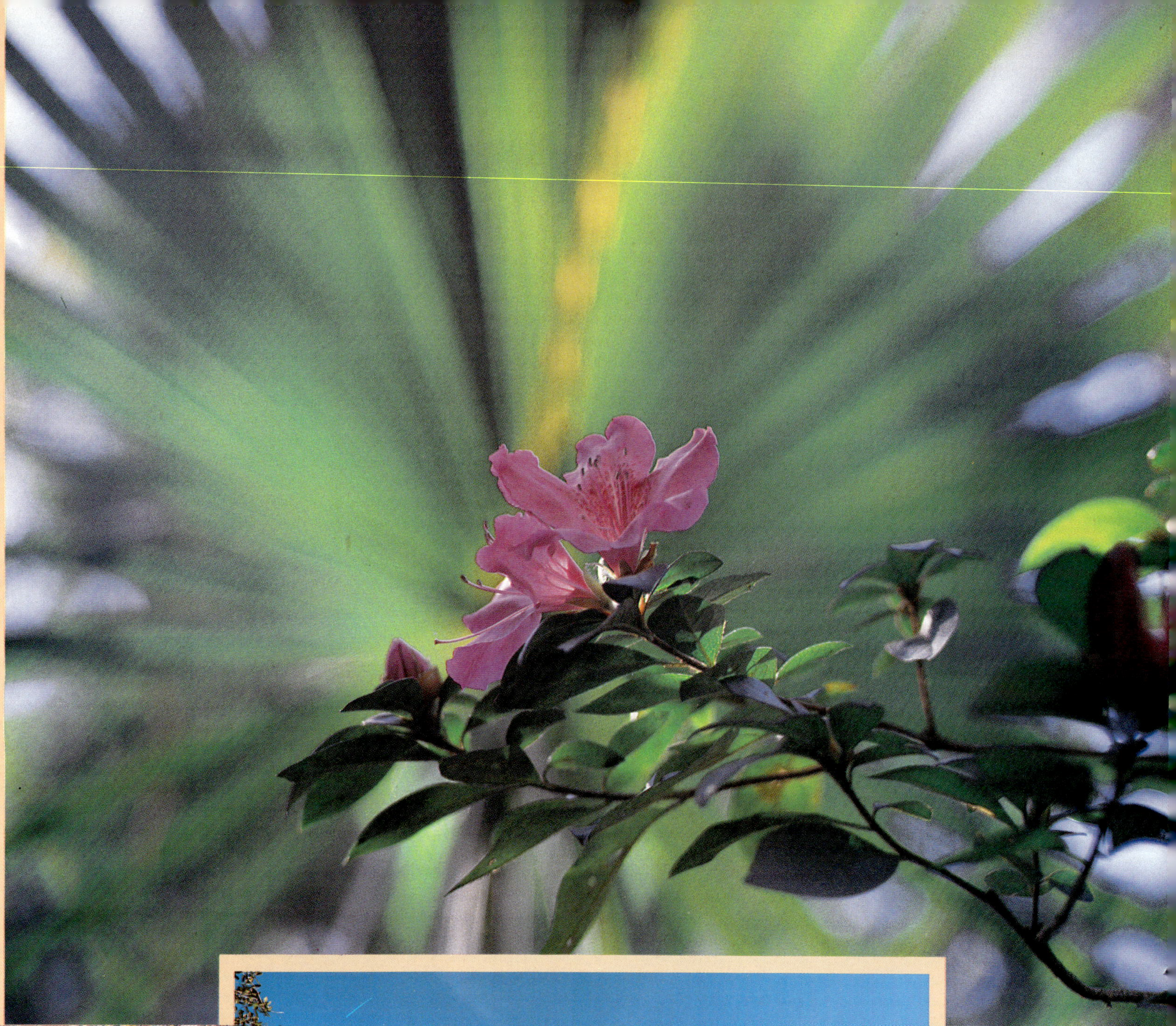

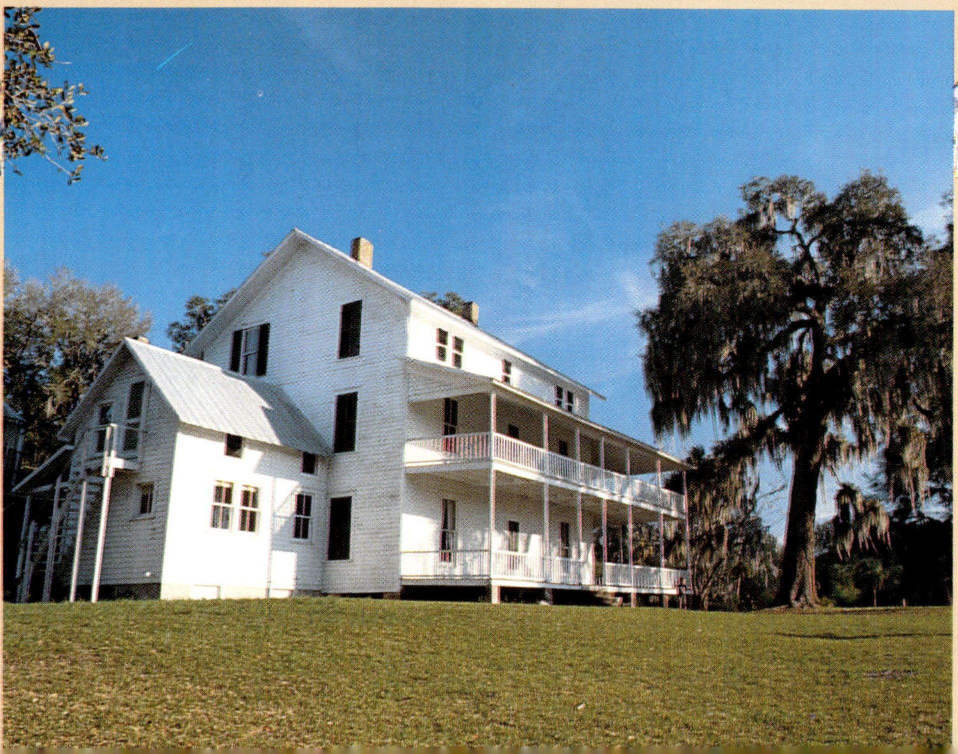

Orlando blooms in Spring, Summer, Winter and Fall. The Thursby House, circa 1880, at Blue Spring State Park, near Orange City in Volusia County.

Blue Spring is a favorite swimming spot for manatees and other visitors. The St. Johns River is a popular spot for boating and fishing.

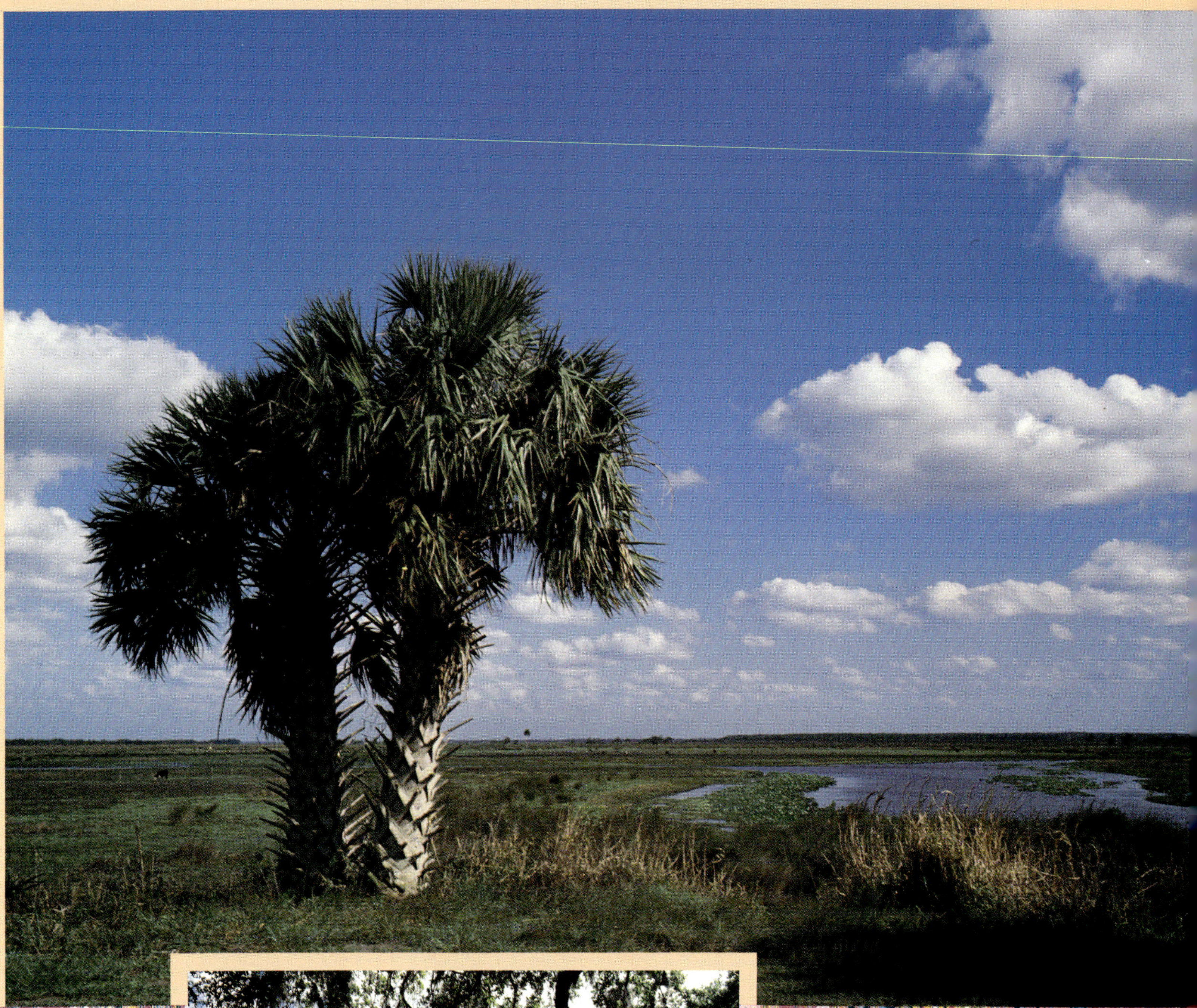

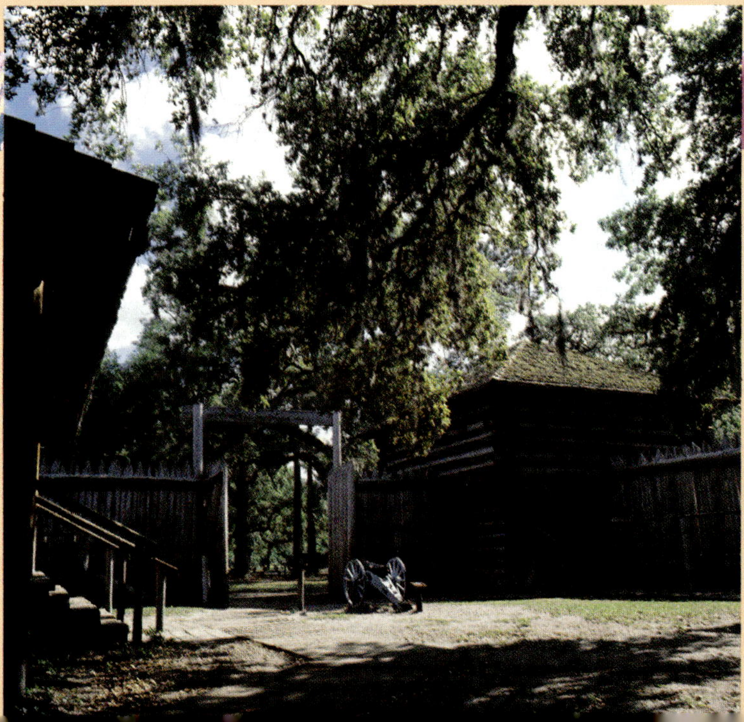

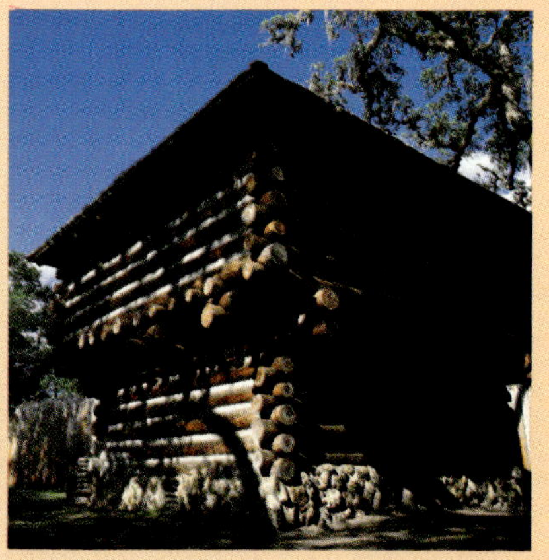

The St. Johns River runs between Brevard County and Orange County at State Road 50. □ In 1837 the U.S. Army built Fort Christmas in Orange County for the Second Seminole War.

Cooling off at Kelly Park. Testing the spring-fed waters of the Wekiva River. Moorings at Sanford Marina on Lake Monroe. □ Exploring can be done by canoe on the Wekiva River or underwater at the Wekiwa Springs State Park.

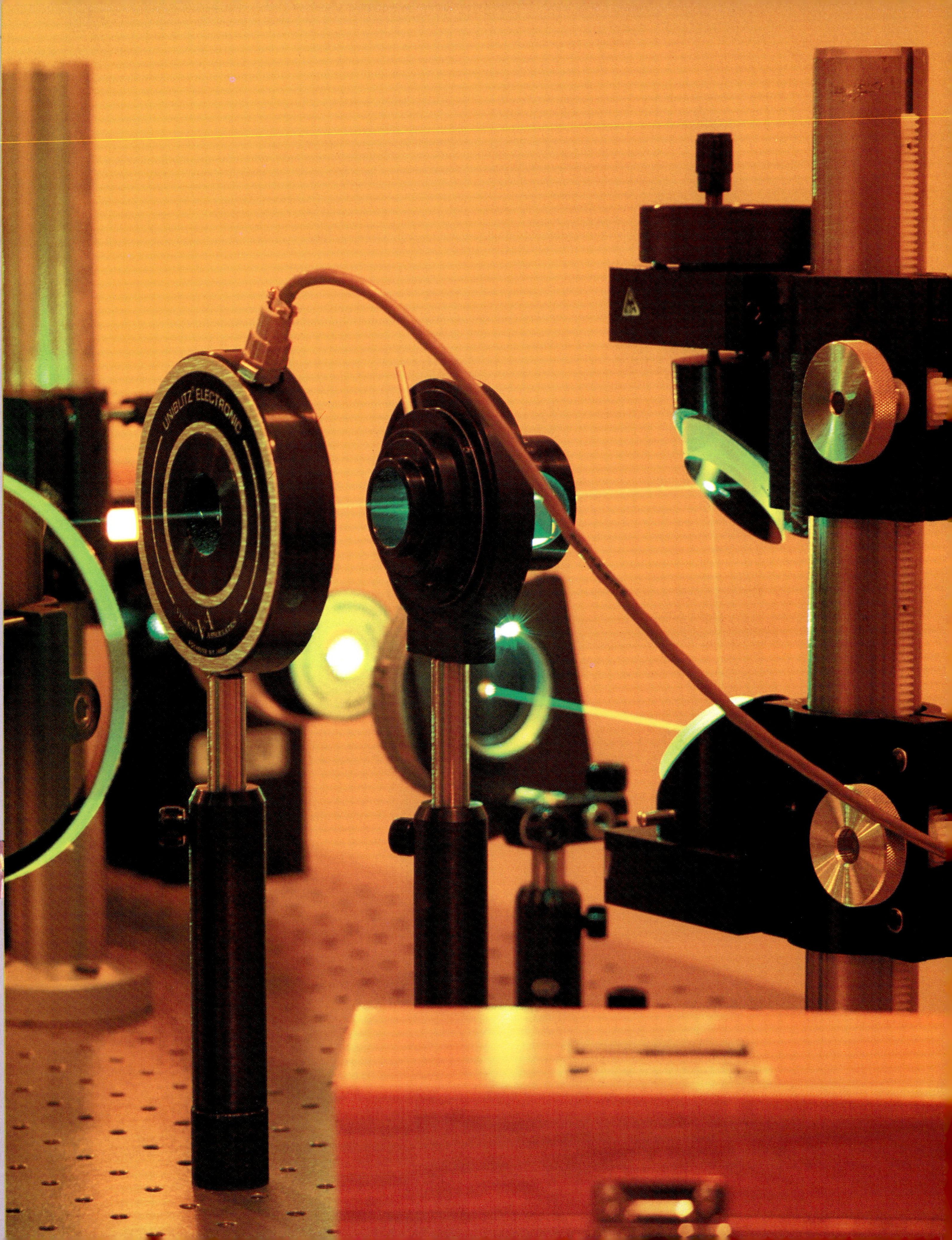
UNIBLITZ ELECTRONIC

Nowhere To Go But Up

Orlando means business. A range of industries — from agriculture to high technology — have started, relocated and prospered under the Central Florida sun.

And all the business growth means growth in housing, retail, employment, transportation, education, health care and finance.

From all indicators, Orlando's business growth is a chart buster.

uture applications for lasers are being studied today
the Center for Research in Electro-Optics and Lasers at
he Central Florida Research Park.

Heathrow, near Lake Mary, is the new home of AAA. About 900 employees work in the new headquarters building.

Cocoa Beach goers watch the launch of a space shuttle.

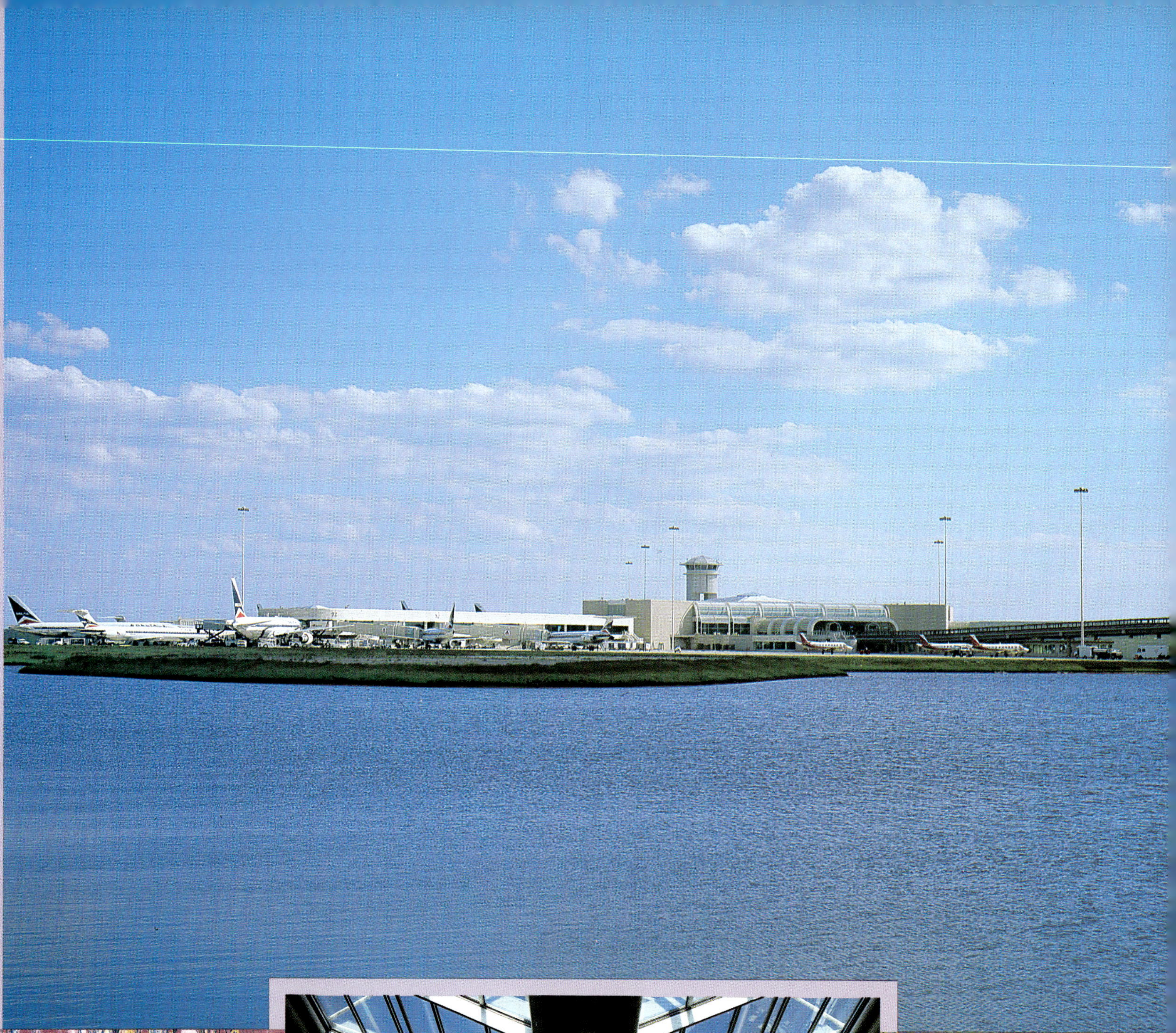

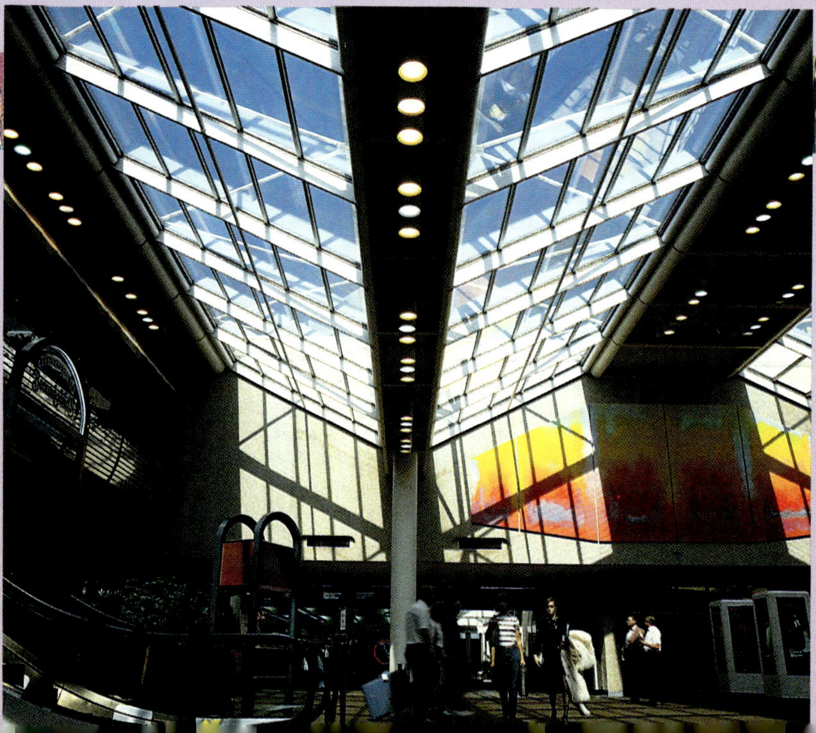

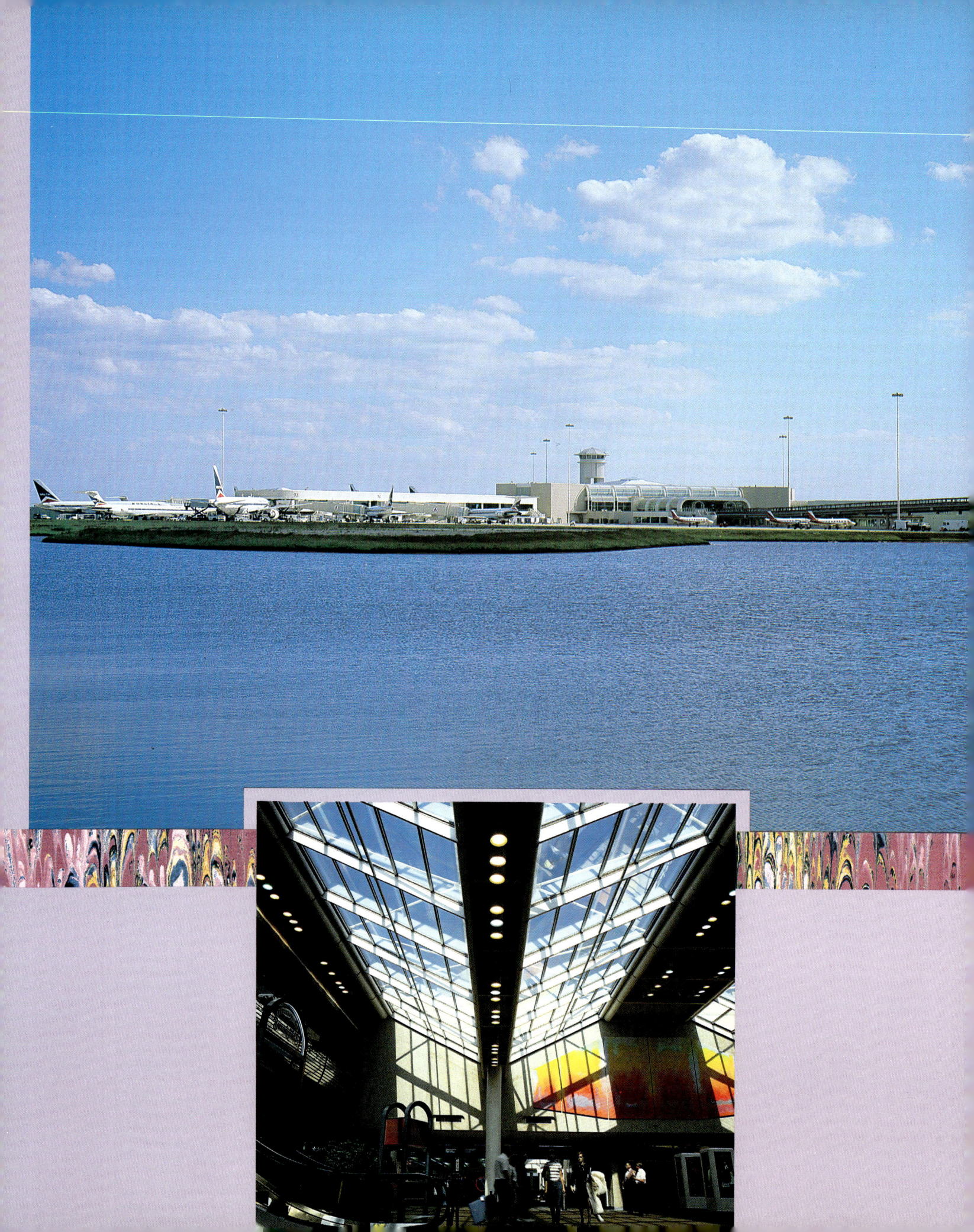

The ever-expanding airport's newest addition is the 24- gate Delta Air Lines flight center. Even the Concorde has taken advantage of Orlando International's modern facilities.

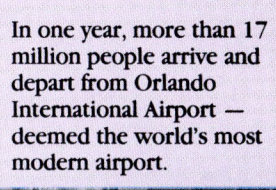

In one year, more than 17 million people arrive and depart from Orlando International Airport — deemed the world's most modern airport.

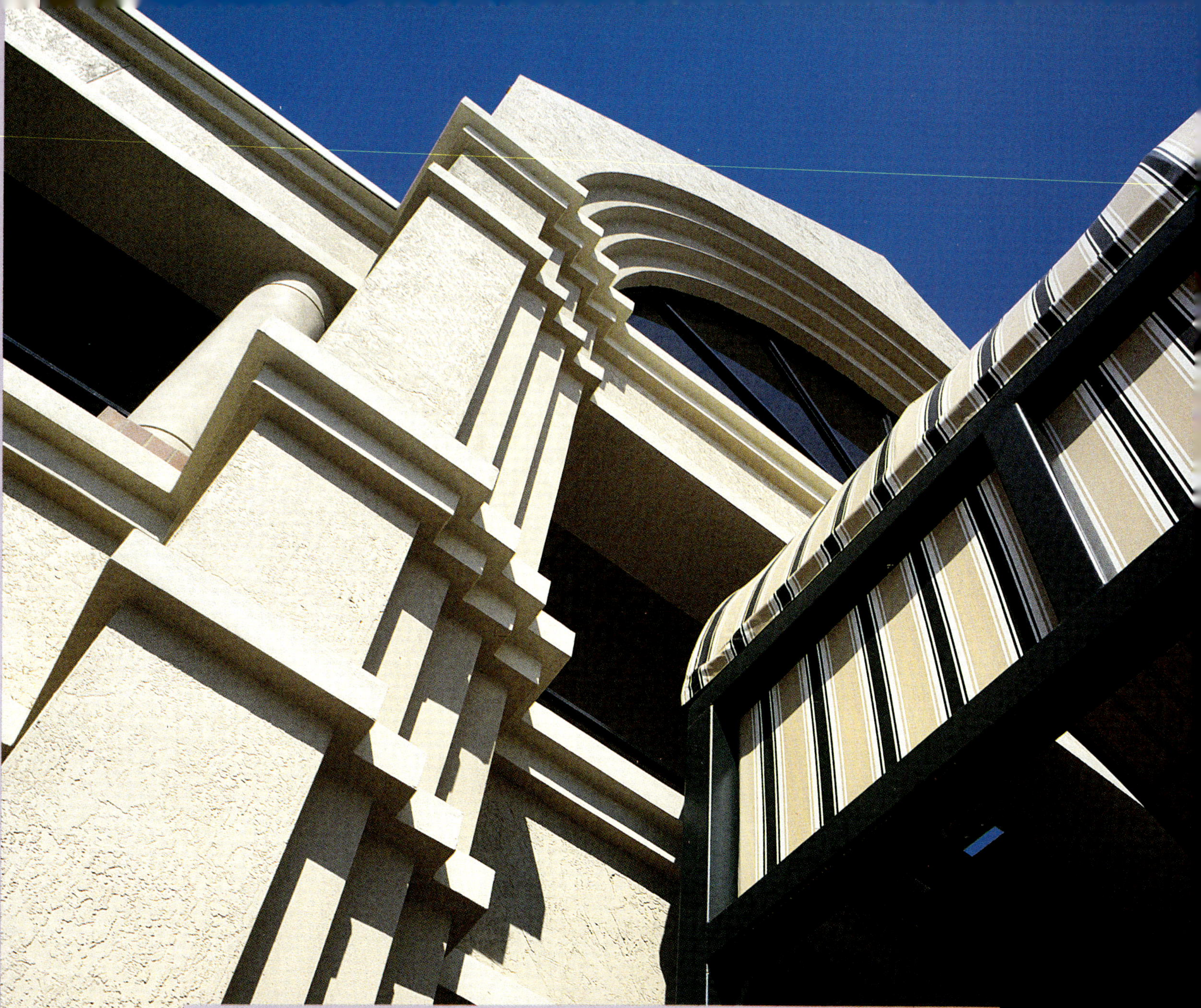

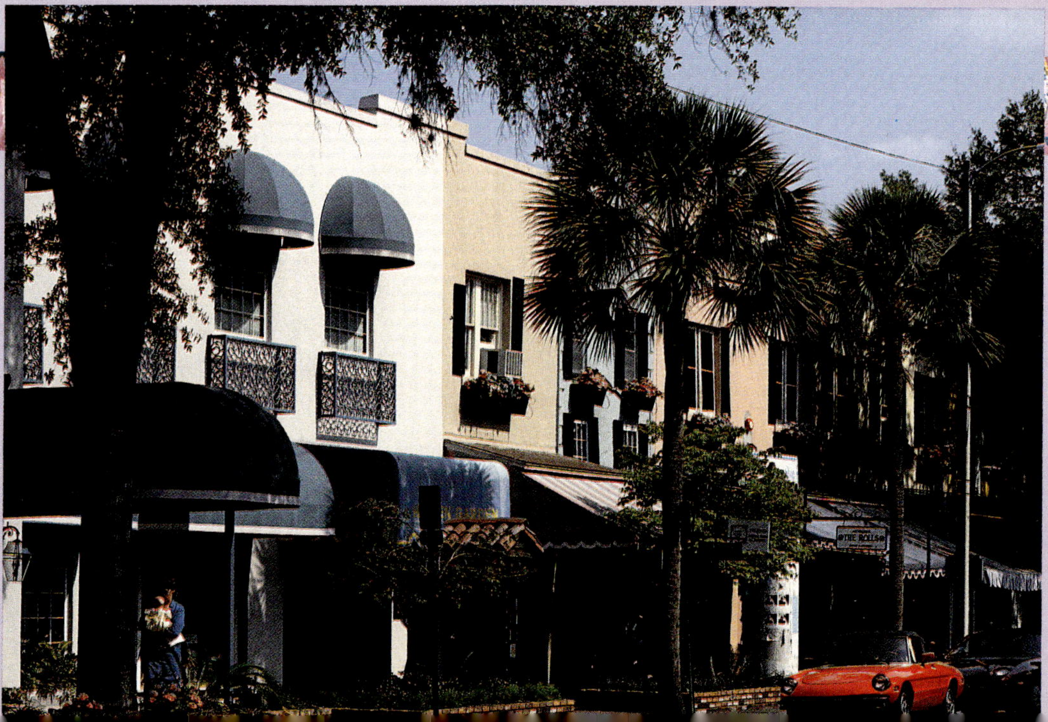

In north Seminole County, The Shoppes at Heathrow offers shopping enthusiasts elegant shopping — including brass shopping carts at the grocery. Winter Park's Park Avenue has tree-lined streets and unique shops and boutiques.

The Exchange is an extension of Church Street Station. ▫ The Marketplace near Bay Hill. ▫ Mercado, in south Orlando, has shops with an international flair. Florida Mall brings the mall experience to south Orlando. ▫ The Exchange shops carry on the historic look of Church Street.

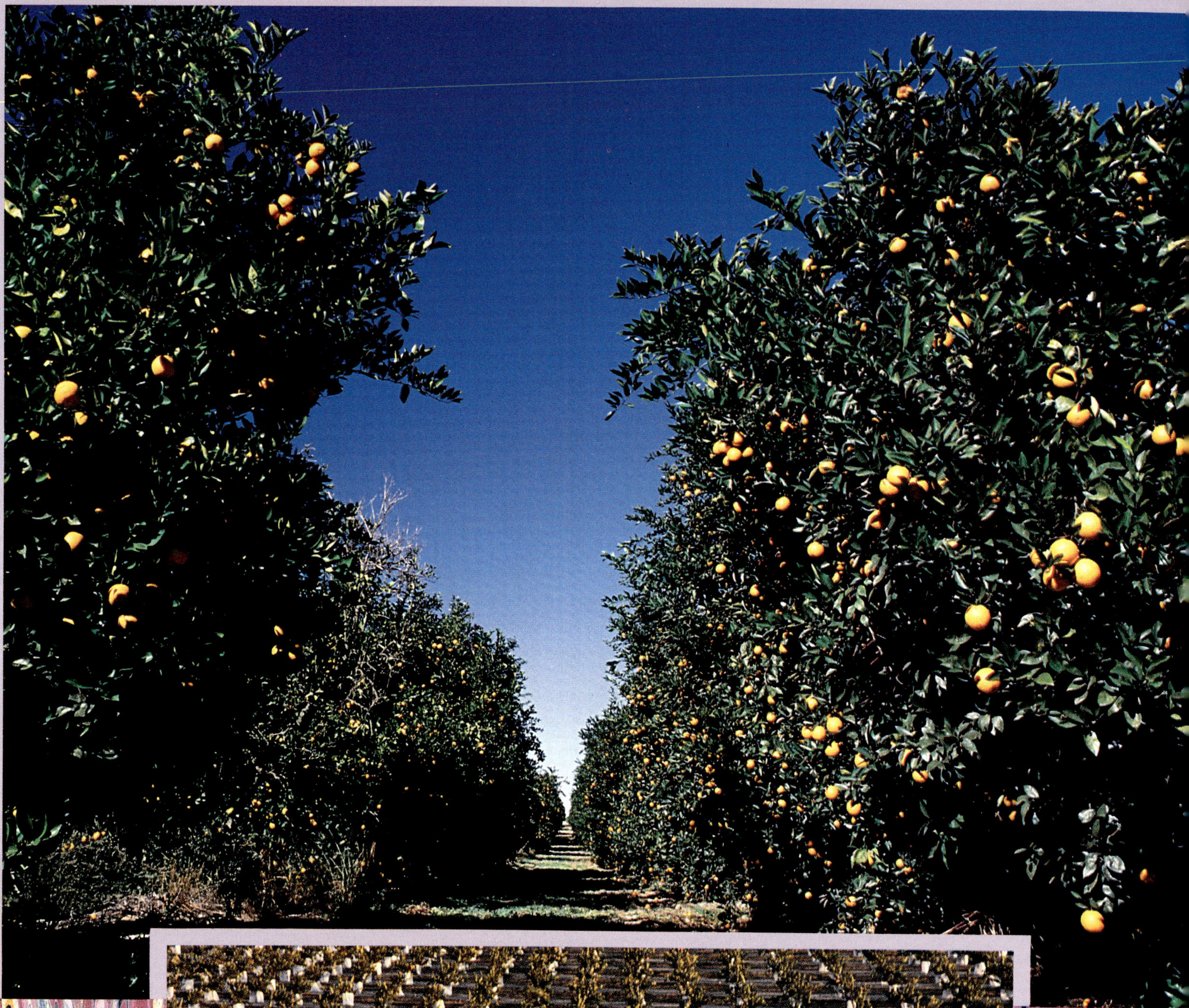
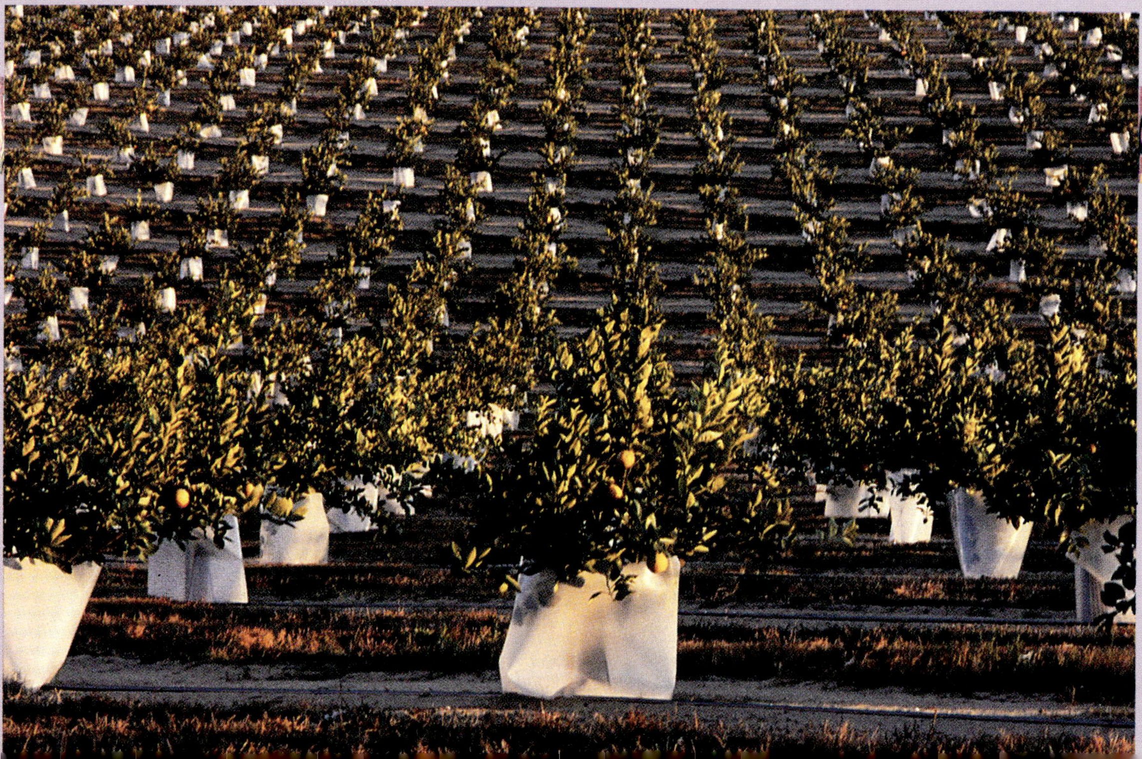

Florida citrus is nurtured in the Central Florida sun. Mature groves bear hearty fruit. New plantings ensure future harvests.

The wares at Apopka's Arts and Foliage Festival. Vineyards thrive near Clermont. □ Zellwood is where the sweetest corn in the world is grown.

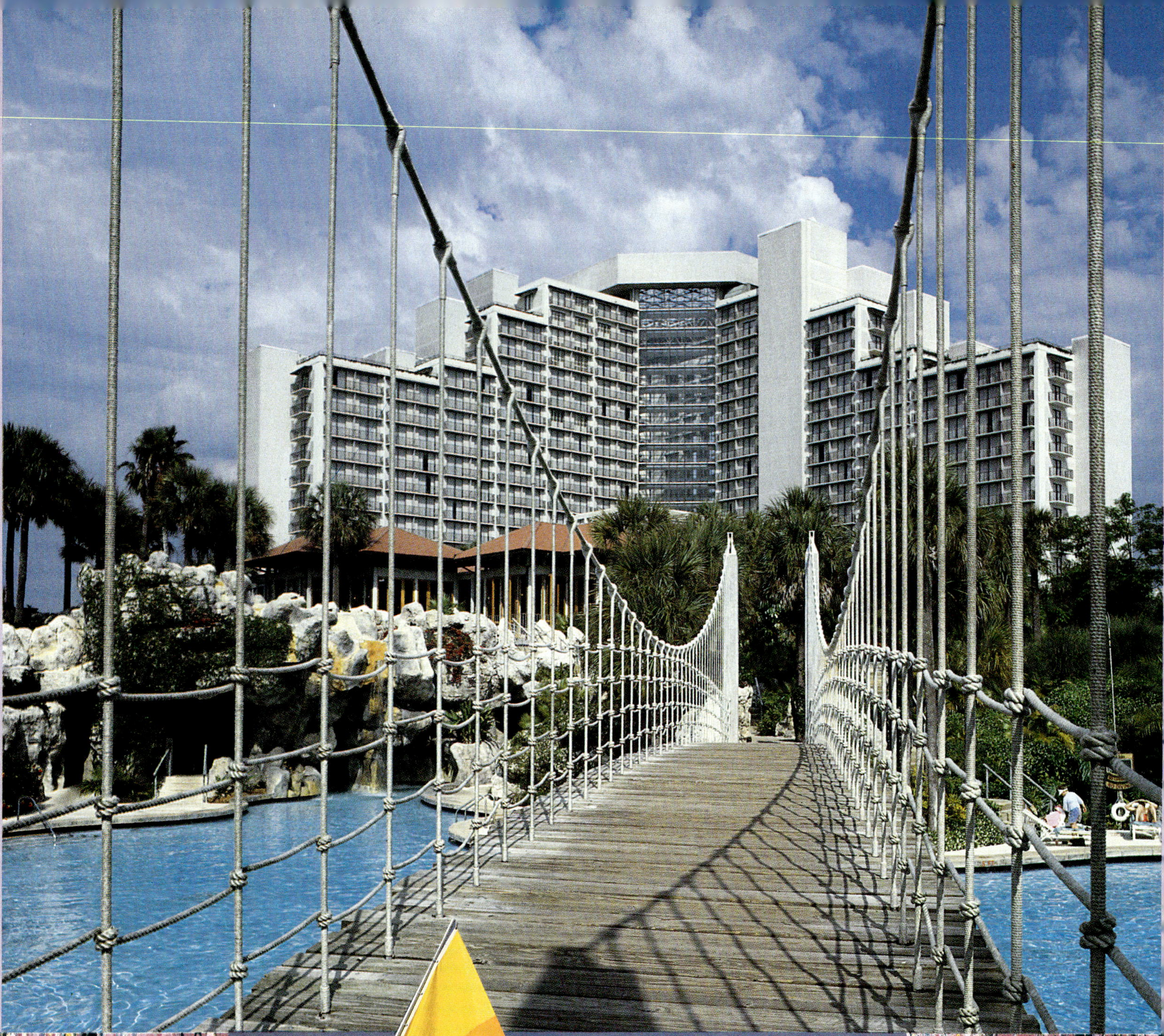

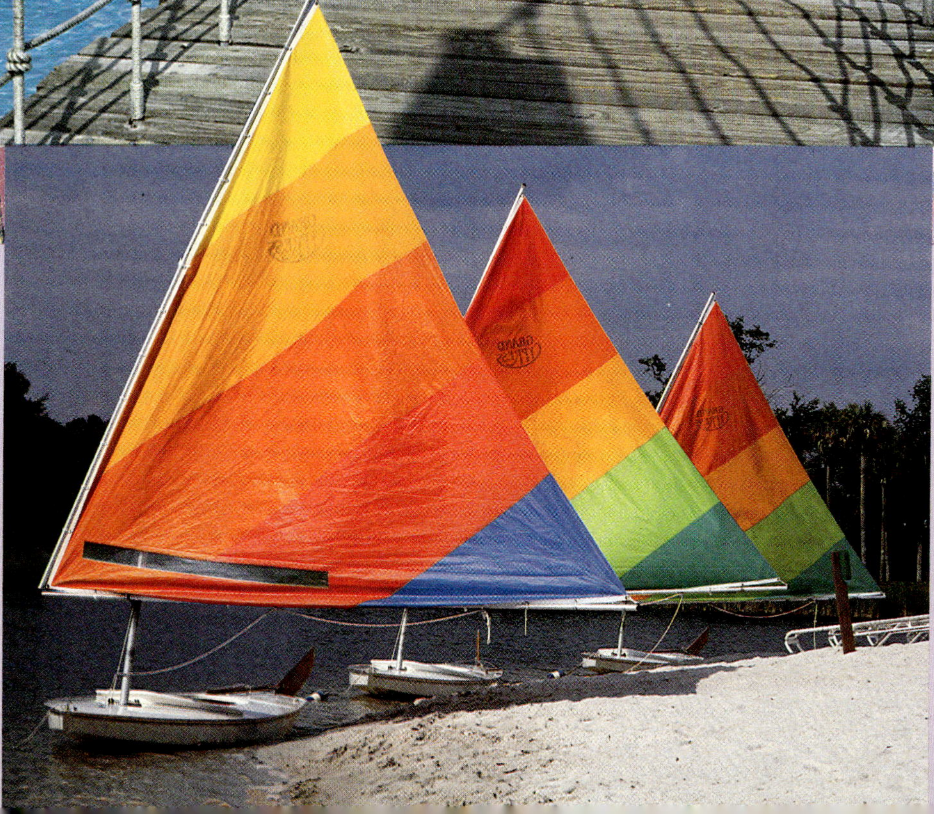

A swinging bridge spans a half-acre pool at the Hyatt Regency Grand Cypress, a luxury hotel in south Orlando. The resort also offers a Jack Nicklaus signature golf course, tennis courts, equestrian center, health club, racquetball and lake sailing.

The Peabody Orlando on International Drive. Across the street, Orange County Convention/Civic Center. □ A bird's-eye view of International Drive and the Wet 'n Wild water park. Superboy TV series on location at Dr. Phillips House downtown. "Psycho" house at Universal Studios Florida. □ Mickey and Minnie at Disney-MGM Studios.

Photos courtesy Universal Studios Florida© and Disney-MGM Studios©

Knowles Memorial Chapel on the campus of Rollins College, a distinguished liberal arts college in Winter Park. □ In southeast Orange County, the University of Central Florida is a quarter of a century old and already emerging as a leader in the state university system — and in the fields of engineering and computer science.

A sample of the companies making up Orlando's diverse economic base: newspaper publishing at The Orlando Sentinel, Institute for Simulation and Training, Martin Marietta, Naval Training Systems Center, Harcourt Brace Jovanovich, Westinghouse, AT&T, residential construction and the Orlando Naval Training Center.

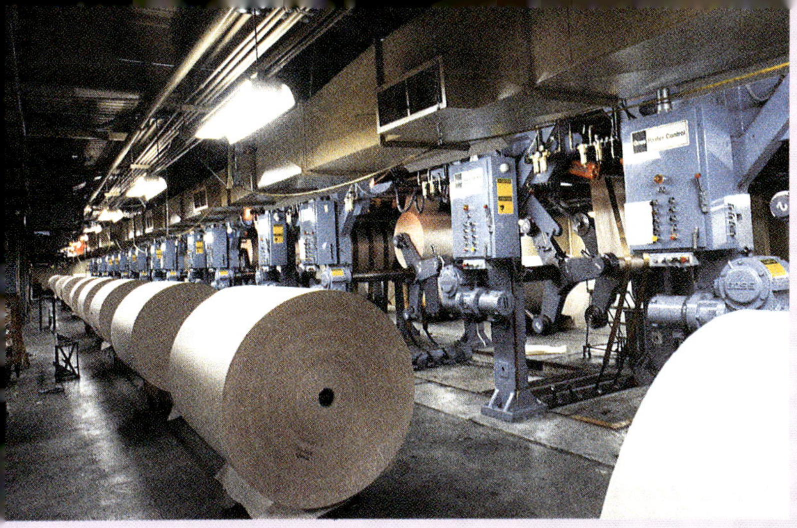
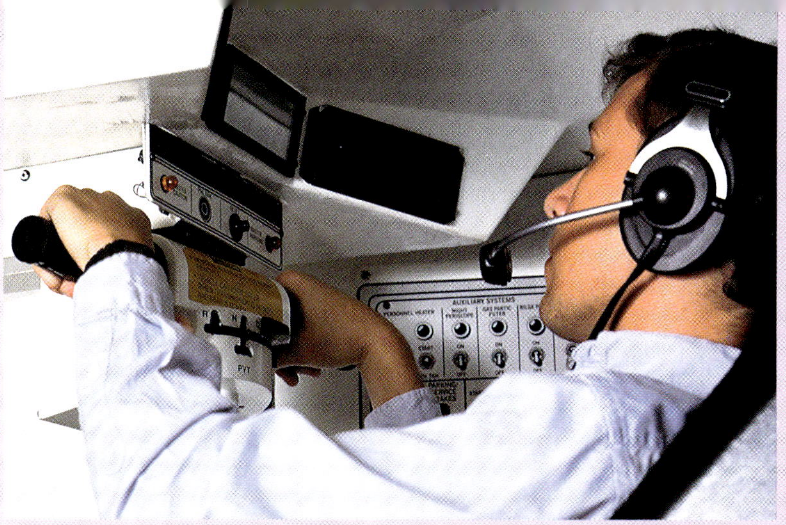
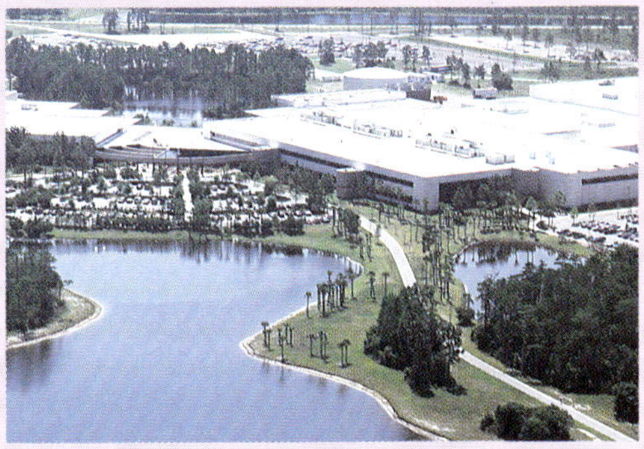
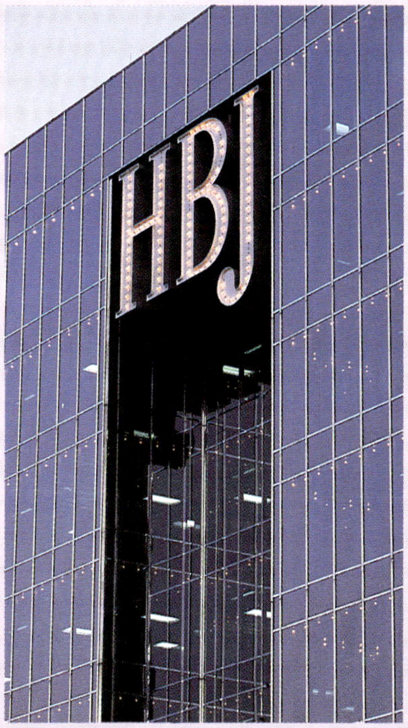
HBJ
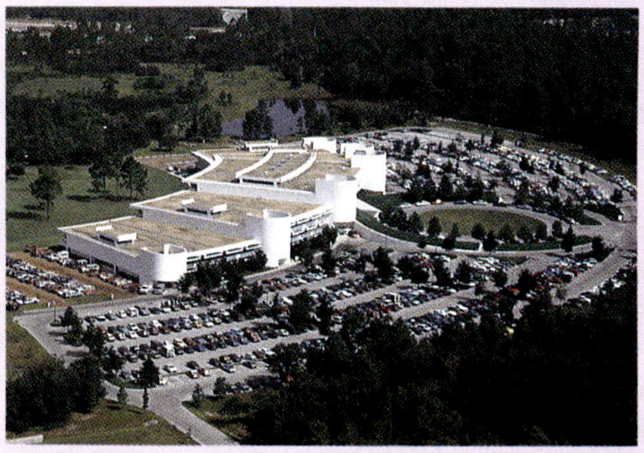
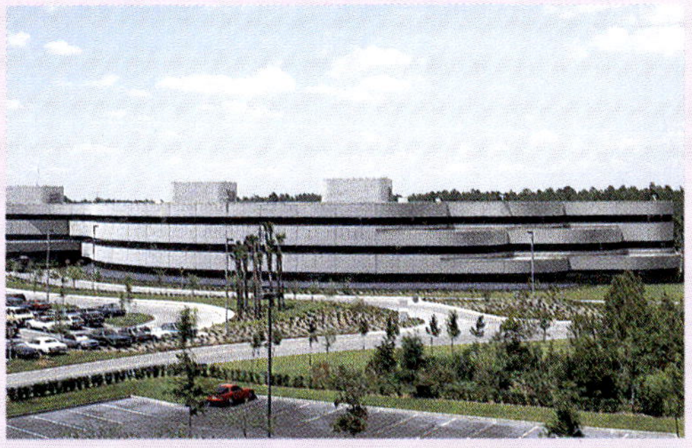
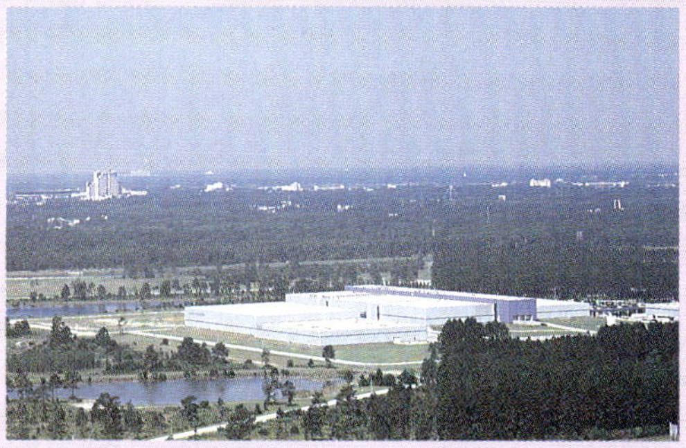
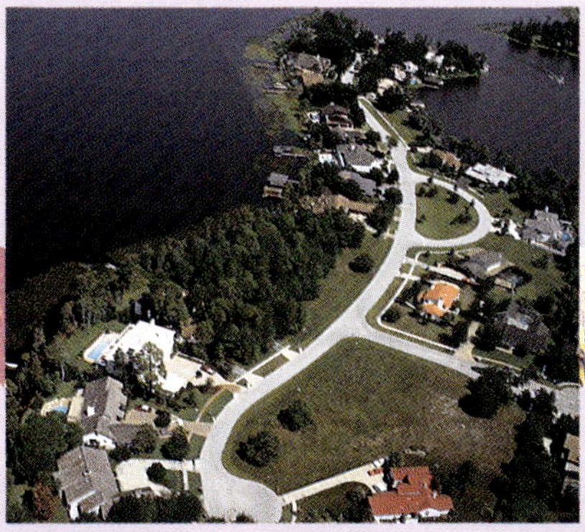
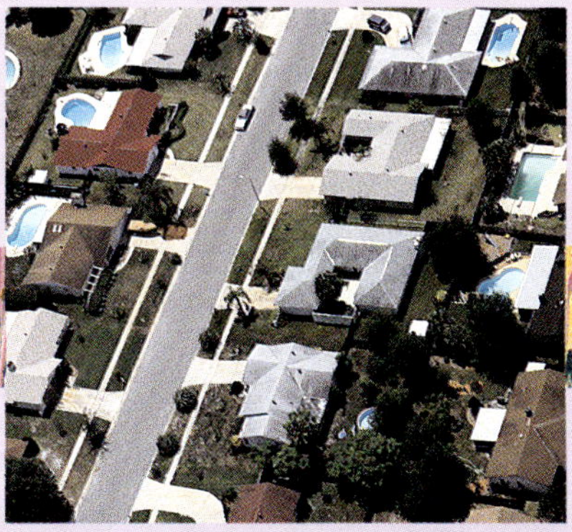
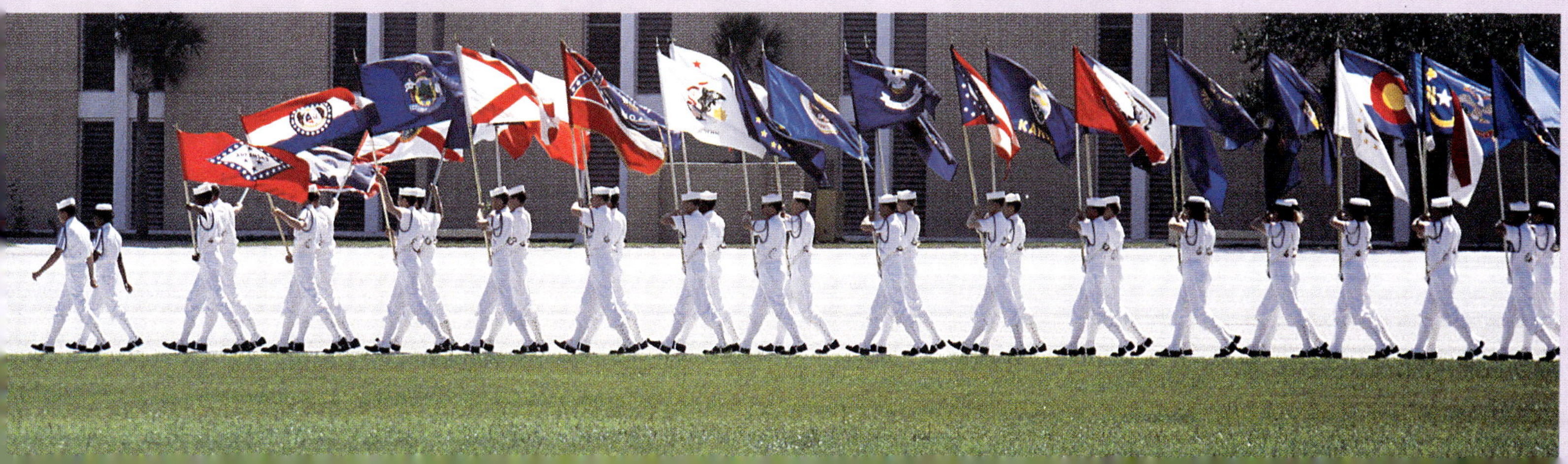

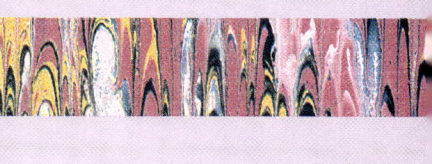

Greenwood Urban Wetland
near downtown.

Clouds are Florida's mountains — as seen from Lake Ivanhoe.